"Miguel clearly lived a full life; fu learning. Poignantly shared and v he extrapolates the life lessons frc simply not visible at the time so t from it too.

Shared openly and from the heart and seemingly leaving no stone unturned, what struck me is his determination to give meaning to (his) life which reminds me of Victor Frankl who said *'Ultimately, man should not ask what the meaning of his life is, but rather must recognize that it is he who is asked. In a word, each man is questioned by life; and he can only answer to life by answering for his own life; to life he can only respond by being responsible.'*"

It's a read as easy as it is deep and wide, as fast moving as it is deeply moving, and as touching as it is light, it left me churning in some places and chuckling in others."

Bennie Naude: International presenter, trainer, coach, facilitator of change & workshop leader.

"Stepping Stones in the Mist is a beautiful, raw, inspirational story about life and the challenges we all have to face sometimes. Miguel takes you on an emotional journey to a place you have never been before and tells you about his life, his torment, his battle, his success. Everyone who reads this book will connect with and learn something new from one or more of the different aspects of life he writes about including addiction, violence, love, loss, separation, illness, vulnerability, joy, beauty, heartache and pain."

Melinda Tizzard: 'Survivor and Thriver'

"This book is a remarkable and graphic account of facing and overcoming many personal life challenges. No wonder Miguel is so well equipped with the necessary empathy, understanding and confidence to help others in the way that he does."

Roger Orgill MBE.

13.5-12.

Matt,
I love you,
you are a beautiful man.
Enjoy the book.
With Love
Miguel

STEPPING STONES IN THE MIST

LIFE LESSONS FOR

OVERCOMING ADVERSITY

MIGUEL DEAN

Stepping Stones in the Mist
Life Lessons for Overcoming Adversity
Copyright © 2012
Miguel Dean
ISBN 978-0-9570973-4-6

Published by KatGab Publishers
Kent, United Kingdom
www.katgabpublishers.com

Author Coach – Will Thomas
Front Cover Design by George Birch
Back Cover Designed by KatGab Publishers
Proof Reading by Melinda Tizzard

Dedication

This book is for all visionaries, healers, artists, pioneers, agents of conscious evolution, way showers, bridge builders, lovers and my mum.

'Be the change that you wish to see in the world.'

Gandhi

Contents

Acknowledgements

Heartfelt gratitude to all of the following people;

Without you this book would not have happened.

Paul Hutchins, Will Thomas, Jenneke Pybus, Lissy Lou, Benny Naude, Emily Turnbull, Amanda Arnold, George Birch, Caroline Staunton, Rose Langham, Cath MacDermott, Laura Buckingham, John Lee, Nick Williams, Robbie Austrums, Helen Worral, Katrina Turnbull, Roger Orgill, Vicky Ross, Lisa Honey, Julie Umpleby, mum, dad and anybody else who I may have forgotten.

Thank you

Disclaimer

All the names of people in this book, to preserve their privacy, have been changed, apart from those who have consented to me using their real names.

There has been no intention to offend or hurt by what I have written in this book. My wish has been to retell what happened and I am aware that this is subject to my own recollection and interpretation of events. These may differ to those of other people mentioned in the book.

Foreword

In this book, Miguel Dean has done a rare and beautiful thing, he has stripped himself bare, to tell a warts-and-all-story, that is both authentic and deeply inspiring. They say that vulnerability is the key to change. Taking your darkest secrets and telling them to the world has a liberating effect on you and others.

Brene Brown, Research Professor at the University of Houston Graduate College of Social Work, has devoted her ten-year academic career to the exploration of vulnerability. She has studied the relationship between shame and vulnerability in the human psyche and drawn some most interesting conclusions. In study, she found common themes emerging about basic human needs. Her starting premise was that all people want to feel connected to other people. It is connection that makes us human and is core to our life purpose. The emotion of shame is really the fear of disconnection. When we fear not belonging, we feel shame. That which we keep from others, we fear will bring about that disconnection.

Her study took her to explore the attitudes of people who did not feel shame in their lives, they were very connected to other human beings. She calls them the "Whole-hearted" and she characterized their attributes as Courage (in its traditional sense of telling others who you truly are), Compassion towards self and others, and Connection through being totally authentic with others. In short these people embraced vulnerability, showing and sharing themselves openly and behaving authentically with others.

This level of vulnerability is not only deeply connecting for the person doing it. It is also connecting for those around.

It is the essence of how great rapport is built. Such openness has the power to connect, and also to heal. The sharing of your story normalizes secrets and erases the shame in others. In Miguel's story, he leads us to insights which can profoundly alter the way we deal with adversity. All human lives contain struggles. Struggles of conscience, loss, grief, sadness, fear, stepping outside of comfort zone, illness, errors of judgment and betrayal, to name but a few. Miguel's story is pure honesty. His soul-bearing will touch you and heal you. His insights will fortify and inspire you. I have not met before such a principled and gentle man as Miguel. He has lived through so much and as such, his wisdom extends way beyond his chronological age This book tells the story of a triumph of a boy who ran off the tracks and found his way to an entirely new and vital life, making a difference and becoming a truly authentic man. He will be the first to say that his journey is not over, that his striving for authentic masculinity in a changing and often confusing world goes on. However he models beautifully as a writer and in his daily life a workable approach to happiness and fulfilment.

At that point we let go of controlling, blaming, perfecting and pretending in our lives, we are vulnerable. At that point there are no walls and no moats, and there becomes no reason for others to attack, moreover there is every reason for others to connect. Letting down our barriers heals us, and others, it builds relationships and sets us free.

This book is about how to let go of fear. Beyond the fear there is always freedom and his story and the insights that emerge from it, are the embodiment of Courage, Connection and Compassion.

Will Thomas - Best-selling and Award-winning Author, of twelve books in the fields of coaching, leadership and creativity.

Introduction

By the time I was five years old it was as if I had lost my mother three times.

My Spanish mother, Natividad, who gave birth to me, died of cancer and never saw me reach my first birthday. I sometimes wonder what it must have been like for her as she lay in her hospital bed and handed me back to my father or a nurse for the last time, knowing that she would never see her little baby again. I wonder what words she said to me then. I will never know, but I am sure they were words of love and in my quiet moments I sometimes feel the whisper of her love deep within me.

After my mother died my father had no choice but to send me to live with my aunt and uncle. My two sisters and my brother were cared for by other friends and family whilst my father continued to work to earn money to pay the bills. I spent about a year with my aunt and uncle and I now know I was loved unconditionally by them as their first born. I am extremely grateful for the time I had with them.

About a year later my dad remarried and our fragmented family was reunited - being separated from my loving aunt was my second early experience of loss.

My new stepmother was also Spanish and it was with her that I have my earliest memories. The first was of being stung by a wasp while collecting windfall apples in our back garden. Perhaps this was one of my first lessons: **that life in all its amazing beauty also involves pain**. My second memory of my stepmother was when I was four and I remember placing my ear to her belly to hear my half-brother inside her womb. Little did I know that this would be the beginning of losing my mother for the third time for, as her first born, her new baby would be the apple of her eye and the focus of her love.

I remember little of my childhood, but I know the overall picture was not a happy one. As a child my life was scary. My stepmother was often angry and this erupted into physical violence.

~

I remember a time in my thirties when I was teaching a group of homeless sector employees. The topic we were exploring was abuse. Standing at the front of the room I had written on the flipchart the different types of abuse: physical, emotional, psychological and sexual. As I stood there and asked my students to give examples of the different types of abuse they had encountered, it struck me in that moment, that although I had never been subjected to sexual abuse, the rest had all been significant parts of my childhood. As you can imagine, the timing of this realisation was not ideal and although I held back the tears I was drawn to share my realisation with the group. I see now that this experience was guiding me towards the place where I now find myself sharing my story with you - my vulnerability, my experiences and adventures - in the hope that it may help and also give hope to others who have been through, or are going through, challenging times.

~

My childhood was not all dark. I have memories of wonderful holidays in Spain, magical Christmases with my cousins, wild adventures in the countryside, building dens and roaming freely with my dog; jumping off hay bale stacks, badminton games in the garden with my sister and hours of football with my friends in the village. However, as I look back, the overriding feelings that prevailed were of fear and anxiety. When I was upstairs in my bedroom and my stepmother called my name there was always a feeling of dread. What had I done wrong? Had she found out about something? Was I again to face her cutting words or perhaps worse?

My dad was not at home much. He always seemed to be at work, or at the allotment, or later on out running. He did his best and worked hard to earn a living so that he could support his family. As a child I couldn't understand why he didn't protect us from the rage and anger of my stepmother. Until recently a frightened little boy inside me would sometimes appear unexpectedly, but I have learnt over the years to be reassuring and loving with him and he rarely shows up now.

~

School was ok - I was an average student. I did my best but struggled to retain information which had a big impact at exam time. As a result of what was going on at home it is not really surprising that, despite my efforts, I was always struggling to focus on my studies and I achieved only average grades in my exams.

Apart from my struggle to do well in my academic studies I am also aware I found it hard to fit in with my peers. There was a lack of belonging that overshadowed me in my school years. I never really felt the same as the others. Desperately I wanted to be cool and accepted, but in order for this to happen I always had to be false, and this did not feel good. It didn't help that my parents insisted I wear the most uncool clothes to school! Changing my clothes secretly behind some rhododendron bushes on the way to school and on my return journey became a daily occurrence. Every day I lived in fear that I would be discovered and punished for my crime. My parents never did find out. I wonder if those bushes are still there. They served me well.

On leaving the sports hall where I had sat my last A-level exam I remember saying to myself 'I was finished with learning' and I would never read another book in my life. The exam experience had been so stressful for me. If this was learning then I wanted nothing to do with it. However, because I did not know what else to do and it was expected of me by my parents, I applied for a deferred place at university, though I never really thought that I would actually attend. Even though Sunderland Polytechnic accepted me to study Combined Arts, my heart was set on a new type of education, an education in the University of Life.

~

At the same time I left school, my father left his job managing hospitals in Stafford to take up a new post at The Royal College of Nursing. This meant we moved to Oxford, where my stepmother had family and dad could easily commute to London. My objective now was to get as far away from my unhappy and oppressive home life as I could - and as quickly as possible. Now that I was eighteen I felt for the first time in my life I had real choices. I quickly found myself a job in McDonalds, with the sole objective of saving money and going to Israel to live and work on a kibbutz. I worked all the hours I could and soon I had enough money for my air fare and more. Just before I left I remember my stepmother suggested I get my hair cut, and for the first time I said no to her. Even though I had been used to doing what I was told, this time I did not. My plan was to grow my hair long and wild. It was a significant point in my life, one of the many of which were to come and, for the first time, I was beginning to realise: it was up to me. It was really up to me whether my hair was long or short, what clothes I wore, what food I ate and what I did with my life. After all, it was my life now and not that of my parents. By this time I had been listening to my heroes Bob Dylan and Pink Floyd for a couple of years already and I had begun to get a faint whiff of the freedom that some of their songs alluded to.

~

So, those were my early years - the days when I was a passenger in the vehicle of life. I know my parents did their best with the knowledge that they had at the time and in the circumstances they found themselves in. We are all products of our upbringing and neither my father nor stepmother had had an easy time growing up. I cannot imagine what it must have been like for my dad to lose the woman he loved, the mother of his four small children. It must have been tough also for my stepmother to raise four small children on her own, who were not hers.

~

It is sometimes hard to understand why things happen as they do. What I do know is: it is not what happens, but how we deal with it and what we learn from our life experiences; and to what extent and how quickly we see the gifts in the adversity that we face - this is what is valuable to us...

... and that it what this book is about. It is about the adventures I have had, the challenges I have overcome and what I have learnt in The University of Life. It is about my journey from there to here. It is primarily about the lessons life has gifted me with. It is about the realisation that no matter what hand of cards you are dealt, those are the cards you have to play in this game of life. There is no point in wishing you had been dealt a couple more aces. The cards you were dealt are what you have to work with. When you realise that you can make your own decisions and make your own choices; then your destiny really is up to you. It is at this point you can shuffle over into the driver's seat of the vehicle that is your life, take the steering wheel firmly in your hands and decide your own destiny.

What you do with your precious time on this earth is your responsibility. My responsibility at this time of my life is to share what I have learnt from some of my own key experiences. I will share with you my life of drugs and violence, love and separation, illness and health, struggle and pain, connection and beauty, and how all of these things have brought me to the privileged place where I now am - the choices we make, in what we believe, or think, or do - they are our choices. My choices began when I climbed onto the bus heading for Heathrow airport, with my uncut hair, my rucksack and a ticket to Israel in my pocket and from that moment on my destiny was in my own hands.

Chapter One - Unconscious Rebellion

I met my first real girlfriend when I was in Israel. Her name was Fay and it was no time at all before I was under her spell. She had long, brown, wavy hair, dark brown eyes, and a huge smile that revealed cute dimples in her rosy cheeks. Our time together was short, but I still have fond memories of her, and can clearly see her smiling face. I did my best to lose my virginity to her; however, a combination of my inexperience at that time and the 'time of the month' meant that it never quite happened. All too soon she returned to England and I was left to grieve her absence.

I left the kibbutz not long after, and wandered around Israel for a while, spending much of my time in Jerusalem. One day, whilst I was in the old quarter of the city, I was approached by a man. He said that I looked a bit down on my luck and offered to buy me a meal at the nearby church. I guess I saw the world as quite a dangerous place at this time but I decided that I would keep my wits about me and cautiously accepted his offer. True to his word, he bought me a meal that I enjoyed. He talked a little about his Christian faith but he did not try to force anything on me. When I had finished eating he shook my hand, wished me well and was gone. I did not expect to ever see him again and was surprised when we met again four years later.

I was on a tube train in London and the carriage was rather full. There was, however, one seat that was only occupied by a bag of onions. I asked the man who was sitting next to the onions if he would be kind enough to move them. As he looked up I recognised him as the man who had bought me the meal in Jerusalem! He recognised me too, and we briefly exchanged pleasantries before the tube came to a stop, and he left. **Life is**

full of lessons when we open our eyes and ears and are receptive. Often the lessons are highlighted through synchronicity or meaningful chance encounters [1](also known as serendipity). I believe this experience was to challenge my view of the nature and motives of people. What were the chances of me meeting this man again? To be on that same tube as me, in that carriage at that exact time with his bag of onions? Perhaps my second meeting with the onion man was to bring my awareness to the fact that **there are many good people in the world and, regardless of my past experiences, I should be open to this possibility.** [2]

~

When I returned from three months in Israel, where I had discovered the world of alcohol, women and menial labour, I spent a while living in a flat in Wolverhampton. My brother's friends were introduced to me, and my initiation into the world of illegal drugs began. They were good days. The drugs worked splendidly! I was a rebel. I was free. I was doing exactly what I wanted to; which, just by coincidence, was exactly what my parents did not want me to be doing! There was a good alternative scene in Wolverhampton. Long evenings in pubs usually ended in even longer nights at friends' houses or impromptu parties, where the sole objective was to get as 'out of your face' as possible. My friend Billy had an old Land Rover, and we would go away from Wolverhampton on camping weekends - it seemed, mainly, so that we could take drugs in alternative surroundings. After one particularly long afternoon in the pub, we all went back to my flat and somehow a water fight ensued. The landlord was not impressed. Nor were the tenants downstairs, who found that they had large quantities of water running down their walls. I promptly found myself evicted. The obvious course of action was to move in to my friend's flat, and as I had not developed any more constructive plans, I would stay there until it was time to take up my place at Sunderland Polytechnic. Unfortunately my friend's place only had one bedroom, so my bed was in the kitchen. It was a large kitchen and the arrangement worked well.

My place at Sunderland Polytechnic did not last long. Within three months I had been evicted from the halls of residence for smoking cannabis. I moved into a shared house with another couple of dope-smoking buddies and pretty soon it was a rare occurrence for me to be attending lectures. The academic world was again making little impression on me; by comparison, the continued use of cannabis, exploration of LSD, and magic mushrooms was much more colourful. At this point my parents were paying me an allowance on which to live, and I figured out that instead of spending my dad's money, I may as well drop out properly from college and sign on to join the ever-increasing number of unemployed in the north east. Interestingly, my dad never thanked me for saving his money; I think the disappointment of me 'dropping out' resulted in his failure to notice my concern for wasting his money.

Drugs became my first true love in Sunderland, followed closely by a woman named Claire - she was a little older than me, had a car, was wild and was much more experienced in the bedroom department than I was. At the time those factors were important to me; early on in our relationship things became tricky. After the end of her previous relationship her ex-boyfriend had decided to embark on a round the world trip on his motorbike. Sadly, a little into his adventure, he was knocked off his bike by a lorry in Egypt, and died. As you can imagine, this had a massive impact on Claire and our relationship never really fully recovered. I struggled to understand and had little empathy for what she was going through. To make matters worse, I felt rejected by her inability to connect with me; nevertheless, for the next couple of years we stayed together.

Whilst based in Sunderland, every now and then, I would go to London to do agency or labouring work to raise money for the debts I was accruing as a direct result of my love affair with cannabis. The drugs were good fun to begin with. There was a whole air of subversiveness and anarchy which surrounded the drug culture and the scene that went with it. An altered state of consciousness was quite a treat at first, but the problem with pretty much any drug, is that before too long you don't get a buzz anymore, so you just need more and more to feel normal. It wasn't too long before this was the case for me, and smoking just became the norm, a way of life.

I did a lot of hitch-hiking back then, and enjoyed meeting new people who were kind enough to give me a lift. There were a few odd characters along the way, like one man who insisted that I should come back to his place for the night as there were two prostitutes he wanted to introduce me to. I managed to persuade him that, although the offer was very kind, I really needed to get to London as soon as possible. Another guy who gave me a lift was rather intent on touching himself, and when he suggested we pull over and masturbate I let him know that we were stopping at the next services where I was getting out. What he did after that was up to him, and I hope he had a wonderful time. On the whole though, most people who gave me lifts seemed to be pretty decent folk.

In London I would sleep on friends' floors, or in squats, and live frugally. The work was usually menial and mindless, and the details of each job are not clear now. I do remember one job in particular. I had reported to the Job Agency as usual in the morning to see what treats they had in store for me. Bored to death by the recent work I had been assigned, I asked if they had anything a little different and by chance, on that day, they did. Before long I found myself in the operating theatre of a hospital. My job was to wheel the anaesthetised patients in and out of the operating theatre, move the lights for the surgeons, and clean up the blood and bits after. After witnessing a couple of circumcision operations, and nearly passing out on a number of occasions, I decided that this was definitely not a career path for me! The next morning I was pleased to be back in a warehouse doing mindless, boring tasks.

On another occasion a group of my friends and I went to London for a different reason. It was the day of the Anti-Poll Tax Demonstration. This peaceful demonstration soon developed into a full blown riot, with many casualties on both sides. It was terrifying to be in Trafalgar Square that day. It really was a battlefield. The police struggled against the anger of the uprising protesters, and anyone else for that matter who happened to have had a bit too much to drink on that day. Not being one for violence I didn't hang about too long, although when we regrouped later my friends told of the casualties they inflicted on the enemy that day. I had developed quite a dislike for the police by this time. I guess I saw them as upholders of a system that I did not want to be a part of. They were an easy target for my scorn, and run-ins with them in the future further served to fuel my contempt. At that time I was dressing in combat trousers, big baggy jumpers, ripped T shirts, army boots and sporting my first tattoo. My long blonde hair had been shaved at the sides, I had a Mohawk top and long dreadlocks at the back. I stood out and my message, put politely, was: 'I don't belong to your society, and I reject your values.' I looked intimidating, in the same way as a dog looks intimidating when it's heckles are up because it has been cornered. On some unconscious level I felt life had cornered me. Although I didn't realise it at the time, I was fearful, and the best way to keep people away was by my appearance. On the whole it worked.

Sunderland days continued in a drunken, stoned haze. By this time I was dealing drugs to help support my habit, as one does. I had the odd run-in with other drug dealers, who were not impressed by my reckless decision to start dealing on their patch. But it didn't bother me too much. I didn't care about anything except sorting out my next smoke and I certainly didn't take care of myself. My accommodation also reflected how I felt about myself, and the shared house I lived in soon became a dump. There were smashed windows and broken doors. The upstairs sink in the hall became the men's toilet because we couldn't be bothered to go downstairs. We ripped the gas fire out to reveal an open fireplace, and pretty soon most of the landlord's furniture had been smashed up and burnt.

In Sunderland I began to **learn about the deep human need for belonging.**[3] And for the first time I began to feel I belonged. All my friends took drugs. We wore similar clothes and had wild haircuts, and listened to the same 'fuck the system' music. But deeper than this, I think there was a stronger unifying factor. Our appearance and preferences seemed to have been our own choices, but I now suspect that what really unified us, and drove our actions, was an innate lack of having our emotional needs met during our childhoods.

The need for affection, support, encouragement, comfort and safety whilst growing up are fundamental to the development of a healthy human being. My friends were from diverse backgrounds, ranging from particularly working class to extremely upper class, yet we were all united by our fragmentedness. Our solution to the gnawing emptiness within was to fill the hole with drugs and angry music, and direct our anger and disappointment at a visible enemy - the Government, and those whose role it was to maintain the status quo. I was doing what I needed to do. I had found a sense of belonging, and I was having experiences that were shaping the person I am now.

Another experience that shaped me reminds me of how one little choice or decision leading to action can have such a massive impact on the way our lives unfold. It happened when I went to London to buy some cannabis. I had bought quite a lot and was waiting at Victoria coach station to return north. Anybody with any sense would have made sure they turned up just in time for the bus to avoid hanging about with large quantities of illegal substances, but no, not me. As if arriving at the bus station early was not enough, I committed the ultimate drug trafficker faux pas by smoking a joint with a fellow traveller who I met at the station. Smoking drugs in public is not a good idea at the best of times and whilst carrying large amounts of cannabis is a definite no-no! Anyway I was young, reckless and stoned, and didn't care. Things changed dramatically in an instant when a policeman arrived making his way down the line of people asking questions and looking at bus tickets. I was hit by an enormous wave of paranoia, but knew it would only draw attention to me if I were to leave at this point. So I waited my turn, trying desperately not to sweat profusely, and forget the fact that I was sitting on enough drugs to put me in prison for a long time. When my turn came I answered his questions about what I was up to (without telling the whole truth!), showed him my bus ticket and breathed a huge sigh of relief as the policeman walked away. I have never been so relieved to see a bus pull up as I was on that day. If the policeman had asked to search my bag, as was commonplace for a guy dressed like myself, the course of my life would have been altered incontrovertibly. In the past when stopped by the police I was able to swallow the small amount of illegal substance I had on my person. This time I would have been chewing for a very long time. I made my way back to Sunderland, with a wild tale of how I had stuck two fingers up at the capitalist state and her minions. How differently things could have turned out.

On reflection, it seems plain to me now that every choice or decision we have ever made is linked to where we are today and as a result I now endeavour to act more consciously, as I know **every decision or action I make today will impact on all of my tomorrows.**[4]

Sometimes, when I think back to all I've been through, it's a wonder I am still here. One episode illustrates to me how important it was to numb my feelings with cannabis even if it meant risking my life. On this particular day I was again off in search of renewing my dwindling drug supplies, my friend and I went to Leeds on his motorbike as there was nothing about in Sunderland. These temporary droughts were the bane of a dope-smoker's life. My friend's name was Dick and he considered himself a good mechanic, however, my experience was that he did most of his motorcycle journeys with the AA Relay Breakdown Service. He would often push his broken motorbike down the road and call the AA, of which he was a member. He would tell them that he had broken down on his way somewhere, his motorbike would be winched onto the back of the truck and he would get a free ride to wherever he was going. He certainly did make the most of his AA membership! On this day the engine of his little 125cc was working fine, the only fly in the ointment was that his lights were not. We set off reasonably early in the morning, and felt we would easily be back before it was dark, and the trip would be a breeze. Unfortunately, when we got to Leeds the dealer who was supposed to be supplying the goods had nothing for sale and was awaiting a delivery. Total cannabis junkies that we were we decided to wait a while. Needless to say a while turned into a long while and by the time the goods arrived the light was fading. For some strange reason we decided to make a dash for it anyway knowing that there was no way we would get back to Sunderland before darkness fell. Sure enough, half way up the M1 motorway we found ourselves in complete darkness. In no time, and not really surprisingly, we were pulled over by the police. The officer informed us that he had received a number of calls from motorists who said that they had nearly crashed into a motorcycle that was travelling without lights on. When we told the officer that the lights had packed up on the journey he kindly phoned a breakdown truck which picked us up and took us the rest of the way. Fortunately he didn't ask to see what was in my pockets. He was one of the nicest policemen I have met; I guess he could have saved my life. Perhaps someone up there knew I had work to do, and that work involved staying alive.

Probably the one notable achievement of my time in Sunderland was that I passed my driving test. I borrowed the money off Claire and was lucky enough to pass the test second time. I don't know how I passed, as smoking cannabis does nothing for your memory, and every time I got back in the driving instructors' car it was a bit like getting in for my first lesson. I do remember I would book my lessons for first thing in the morning so I would not be so stoned. My driving instructor seemed oblivious to my blood shot eyes. He was more interested in getting me to pull over to show me his most recent batch of photos of scantily dressed women he had taken. Perhaps it's a north east approach to driving instruction?

Another thing I learnt in Sunderland was that I was insecure. Hardly surprising I guess, considering my childhood, but in those days I viewed it as a weakness as I had no understanding of how childhood would affect the way we think, and feel, and act as an adult. My relationship with Claire was stormy. I was certainly more dependent on her than she was on me. Every time she went away to see her mother or visit friends, I would experience tremendous feelings of abandonment and fear. I would find myself doing my best to anaesthetise these feelings with extra quantities of cannabis, but the feelings were so strong that even this did not work. I was jealous and controlling, and probably not much fun to be around at all most of the time. Claire was no angel either. Another victim of a dysfunctional childhood, she was messed up and unpredictable. I was woken abruptly one morning as she dived onto the bed wielding a pair of scissors uncannily close to my face and screaming like a banshee. I can't remember what it was all about but I probably deserved it. Odd incidents like this broke the monotony of the days in Sunderland which were becoming increasingly predictable and grey.

Claire's free spirit was hard to keep up with at times, and one day she announced she was going to go on holiday to Turkey. She wasn't in the habit of asking my opinion and once she had decided something that was it. I had no money as usual and if I was to go with her I would have to come up with a plan and some cash - fast. Sunderland was not an easy place to find work so again I was forced to set off in search of it. Previously I had worked for an old Irish builder in Oxford, so I rang him up to see if he had any labouring work for me. Fortunately he did, and I headed down. By this time my parents were living in Spain, and I lived in a tent on a campsite outside Oxford while I worked there. It was a long walk into town and back each day as I had no transport and I remember what a lonely time it was. But there is a stubborn side to me and when I decide that I am going to do something I generally see it through. Resilience, determination and perseverance are qualities that were probably beginning to develop within me at this time and they were well needed for the challenges that were to come.

The so-called 'holiday' in Turkey was no picnic. It began with a severe case of diarrhoea; I was confined to the hostel for a couple of days after finding that every short walk would result in an undignified shuffle back to the hostel to shower, and change my underwear. When I did get out and about to explore the country it was severely impacted by the fact that Claire insisted on wearing vest t-shirts and short skirts. This was not a good idea in a Muslim country. I constantly felt under threat as I did my best to discourage the Arab men from leering and touching my girlfriend at every opportunity and this made hitch-hiking rather challenging and stressful too! We decided to have a gentle tour on horseback. At least this was what we thought we were paying for.

On the morning of the 'tour' a man arrived with two huge horses, and indicated that we were free to set off on our own. Neither of us had ridden before but being young and reckless we decided there couldn't be too much to it. We set off up the road into the mountains. Because of the short skirt factor, the lorries that drove past kept blasting their horns and scaring the horses. Claire was already pretty nervous on her horse, and before long she had been thrown off into the ditch. Insisting that it was the fault of her horse we swapped horses. It wasn't long after we had decided to get off the road and follow some old tracks that she was again thrown from her horse. This time she landed badly, sprained her ankle and her horse galloped off over the hill. All of a sudden what had seemed like a good idea had turned into a bit of a disaster. I helped Claire to the shade of a tree, and rode off to try and retrieve the runaway horse, reassuring her that I would soon be back. It wasn't too long before I caught up with Claire's horse. It was in the middle of the main road causing quite a hold up. Eventually, after a game of chase, I managed to grab hold of its reins and made my way back to where Claire was waiting in the shade of the tree. We slowly made our way back down to the town in search of medical assistance for Claire's ankle. The medics were very helpful on the whole, apart from a porter who insisted on staring unashamedly up her skirt while the doctor bandaged her ankle. It was not the best holiday I have ever had and I was glad to get back to England.

~

Not long after I left Sunderland I had an unusual encounter with a glass blower. I don't remember all the details, but I think I was in Durham and, for some reason, I was looking around a working museum. One of the crafts that made up the displays was glass blowing. I remember asking the craftsman if he made glass pipes, which were particularly fashionable for smoking cannabis at the time. He told me that he did not, and for some reason I asked him if he smoked. He gave me a knowing look and told me that he didn't anymore. When I asked why he just said "you'll have to work that one out for yourself." I pressed him further, but he would say no more and I left and for some reason that brief exchange has always stayed with me.

Indeed, in time, I did find out for myself why it was not a good idea to be constantly stoned, but it did take a while. It took a while before the drugs wouldn't work anymore, before the numbness was overridden by the pressure within to release the pain of my past. The time would come when I would have to begin to face my demons and somehow it was as if the glass blower knew this.

~

By the time Claire had finished her degree I was ready to get out of Sunderland. We had been to a few festivals over the summer, and with some money that she inherited, she decided to buy an old Leyland FG bread lorry. It was already converted to live in and as neither of us had seen much of Scotland we decided to head north on a tour around the Scottish coast. When I look back I see that my life has been a little bit like stepping stones in the mist, and heading for Scotland in an old truck just seemed to be the right thing to do. The opportunity arose and I took it. Although, for most of my life, I have had no clear goal of where I am going, I feel as if something has been guiding me and it is up to me to have faith, not focus too far ahead, and just take the next step. Often I am not sure what the next step is, or where it will lead, but when the time is right I find that the mist clears, and the next stepping stone appears for me to step onto. There have been times when I have been impatient for the mist to clear. Sometimes the mist clears unexpectedly, and I do not feel ready to take the next step but I have learnt trust. I am reminded of Elizabeth Kubler Ross' words:

'When you come to the end of all the light you know and are about to step into the darkness of the unknown, faith is knowing that one of two things will happen: there will be something solid to stand on or you will be taught to fly.'

So far there has always been something solid to stand on and I believe that, one day, when I am ready I will take a step and I shall learn to fly. But for now I shall continue on my stepping stones. Perhaps the last stepping stone will lead me to death or perhaps there is no last stepping stone... only time will tell.

Lessons for Life

1. Life is full of lessons when we open our eyes and ears and are receptive. Often the lessons are highlighted through synchronicity or meaningful chance encounters.

2. There are many good people in the world and, regardless of past experiences, one should be open to this truth.

3. Human beings have a fundamental need to belong.

4. Every decision or action I make today will impact on all of my tomorrows.

Chapter Two - New Age Travelling Daze

When I cast my mind back to that grim December night near Edinburgh, with my traveller companion standing menacingly in front of me with an axe raised above his head threatening to do me some serious damage, I realise that sometimes I may have made some rather sketchy choices! As a result of my departure from Sunderland it didn't take long before I was fully immersed into the craziness that is life as a New Age Traveller, and soon I would find myself in these awkward situations quite frequently. Violence and aggression were commonplace on the road. I once witnessed a good friend of mine being beaten about the head with an enormous spanner until his head was repeatedly split open like a tomato. If I had not intervened I hate to think what might have happened and it was made worse by the fact that his attacker was a woman! I spent a long time in the hospital that day while my friend had his head sewn up.

As a boy I found there were times when my dog would get into a fight with another dog and without making a conscious decision I would find myself in the middle, doing my best to stop them and bring an end to the violence. This automatic reaction seems to be programmed deep within me and to this day I occasionally find myself intervening in violent situations between strangers. It is never a conscious decision; I just seem to find myself involved. I do not really understand violence and feel deeply saddened that our inability to express ourselves effectively can sometimes result in people physically hurting each other. As I have said, over the seven or so years that I lived 'on the road' violence was commonplace and by the time my travelling days were over I had been attacked with an iron bar and a baseball bat, the end of my finger had almost been bitten off, I had been threatened with a shotgun, I had my nose broken with a head-butt and was kicked and beaten to the ground a number of times.

Fortunately (or unfortunately), most of the time I was so 'out of my face' on drugs or alcohol (or both), that I didn't experience too much physical pain. Within me, as the years passed, there was a growing sense of unease as the pain from my childhood seemed to be building pressure in an attempt to be expressed. The physical pain I suffered was small by comparison to the emotional pain that lay within me. The pain of loss, abuse, isolation, and loneliness from my childhood, I now realise led me to live a life that constantly affirmed to me that I was of little worth. Those were the days when my pain was growing within. **I now know that this pain and pressure would have to grow more and the stakes would have to become higher before I was ready to take stock of my life and really begin to take responsibility and initiate change.**[1]

When I look back it amazes me how I coped. I have always been a gentle person by nature, and the violence I experienced at home meant I hated violence with a passion. I now know that **when things happen to us as children we often interpret the events as being our fault; that we are somehow responsible for what happened.**[2] The experiences I had as a child led me to believe I was not worthy of love. Like a moth drawn to a flame in some strange way I found myself drawn to a life where fear was always in the background and I can tell you it took quite a while after my New Age Traveller days before I could sleep deeply and peacefully without feeling terror in my body at every noise I heard in the night.

So how did I find myself in this awkward predicament on that December night with only an axe and a psychotic skin head for company? It was another pivotal point in my life and was the indirect result of the decision to head for Scotland with Claire.

But before I would arrive at that pivotal point, I had much to learn about my life before I was ready to move on.

~

One day, a few weeks into our Scottish trip, we were parked up in a lay-by, when a van pulled in and there was a knock on the truck door. It was a scruffy chap who turned out to be a fellow traveller, and he told us that he and his mates were parked up not far from us and were helping a local community to prepare for a 'free festival'. We followed him to the park-up and the beginning of my life on traveller sites began. Individuals, couples and families lived in buses, trucks and caravans dotted about a large car park, nestled amongst Scottish hills. I soon realised that there was a class system in the traveller community, ranging from peaceful, dope-smoking environmentally friendly types, to angry, Special Brew consuming anarchists with little respect for themselves, anyone or anything. The traveller community would have been ideal for an army of counsellors, psychiatrists and therapists, apart from the fact that most of us were busy applying our own type of drug therapy, which had a clear focus on running away from ourselves and dealing with as little as possible. I have no doubt that some travellers were doing what they were doing from the perspective of leading a simple and peaceful existence and had little personal baggage, but my experience was these folk were few and far between.

My first traveller companions were easy going dope-smokers, and this suited me fine. We helped with the festival and it was great. It was a real 'free' festival with no tickets or security guards. It was different to most festivals in that the only way you could get there was by boat. There were all the usual trappings of live music, dogs and fires, with home-made bog-myrtle beer, and enough drugs for everybody. As was always the case at festivals I never got to listen to the bands, or at least I never remembered them. Too many intoxicants meant most mornings began awakening from a hazy stupor beside an outside fire with a bunch of friendly strangers and little, if any, recollection of the night before. Breakfast of beer, cannabis and other illegal substances would soon get the day rolling again.

Other festivals dotted the times I spent on the road, and there were many good times. Most of the good times involved getting inebriated. Sometimes we would gather around the open fire together drinking, talking and getting high. On some sites where I lived there were musicians and impromptu jams would get underway beneath the stars as we danced and sang with drunken abandon. There was often a great sense of community and comradeship that was probably strengthened by the fact we were persecuted by the police and feared and mistrusted by the public in general. Sometimes we would talk of how we would never 'sell out' and move into a house. We would live the wild life on the road forever, and those travellers who did leave the road for more conventional life styles were almost seen as traitors. That said, the good times are not the times that stand out the most. It's funny how often the 'bad' experiences stand out the most - they are often the ones that make us sit up and take note. **I now see that these challenges arose in my life as opportunities for me to learn.**[3]

One such incident that does stand out in my memory is of an unpleasant encounter with a policeman. I realise now it impacted on me so much because it triggered some deep feelings from my childhood. It relates to the abuse of power and to this day it is one of the few things that results in me becoming really outwardly angry. I am aware I am angry at times, but this anger is usually directed inwards, and I find myself being angry with myself for my own shortcomings and imperfections. Twice in my life I have become really outwardly angry, and they were both times when I perceived that someone I cared for deeply had been abused by someone who had misused their position of trust. I suspect this is such a sensitive issue for me because I believe my stepmother abused her power in relation to me and my brother and sisters. As a small sensitive boy what I needed was compassion, love and kindness, but as I have already explained, these were in short supply in the home where I grew up. My stepmother and I now have a good relationship and I hold no malice towards her. She was doing her best and it is no coincidence that as a result of my childhood I have found myself drawn to work with young people who have perhaps not had the easiest start in life. I am good at this work because my own experiences have taught me compassion and empathy. Without having had those experiences I would not have been able to help the young people that I have helped. I am grateful what I experienced has helped me to help others. My experiences of policemen have often been negative and this next encounter didn't help.

A group of us were parked up beside a loch in the north east of Scotland. We were helping to replant the Caledonian Forest. It was hard work. A long trudge up a steep hill with a spade and bags of saplings for company; planting trees, often in severe weather conditions was gruelling and boring work, but it was paid work. One day on returning back to the truck, I found Claire in tears. A police car had come onto the site while we were at work, and one of the policemen had forced his way into our truck. He had intimidated Claire and demanded to know where the drugs were that he assumed she had. When she refused to cooperate, he groped and molested her under the pretence of searching her for drugs. When I heard this I was understandably dismayed and somehow felt that I had failed to protect my girlfriend from the enemy. Poor Claire was in shock but we knew that there was nothing we could do. There had been no witnesses, and it was the word of a 'hippy traveller' against the word of a police officer.

However, as chance would have it, a few days later, as I and a couple of friends were heading into town a police car passed us heading back to our park-up. We made a hasty u-turn and arrived back just as the police were getting out of their car at the site. We never found out what they wanted because we didn't wait to ask. We charged down towards them and I could feel my rage rising. Claire quickly identified one of the policemen as the same one that had sexually assaulted her and he and his comrade quickly found themselves surrounded by a small angry mob. I have never seen such fear in a man's face before, and I had a good view as my face was pressed almost up to his as I hissed out obscenities in an attempt to convey my disgust at what he had done to my girlfriend. I remember my friend shouting, 'throw him in the loch' and for some reason the decision seemed to lie with me. This kind of action was not in my nature. The two policemen were told never to show their faces again. Eventually the crowd parted and they hurriedly clambered back into their car and sped off. I later heard that it wasn't the first time this police man had abused his power with a woman and Claire was asked to give evidence against him in a court case. I don't know whether she did as not long after the incident we separated and she drove off with her new Scottish traveller boyfriend.

~

I know that human beings have the potential to be incredibly beautiful, loving creatures but they also have the potential to be cruel and evil. None of these things happen by chance.

Perhaps the policeman had a messed up childhood but that does not excuse his behaviour. I do find it alarming there are people in authority who can act in such an unconscious way. Among the traveller community there was a rich collection of tales of how police had abused their power. Perhaps they felt that travellers, being a kind of underclass, deserved nothing better.

I don't have an issue with policemen these days. These days I don't have drugs on me and my car is taxed and insured, my MOT certificate is legitimate and I am a law abiding citizen (for the most part). I sometimes feel though that the enforcement of laws means that we can fail to decide for ourselves whether something is right or wrong. I think I understand where Bob Dylan was coming from when he wrote: 'To live outside the law you must be honest.'

~

My haphazard life on the road continued. When Claire left I was heartbroken. She had been my first long term relationship and her departure was sudden. A friend had warned me that she was getting very pally with Scottish Sid but I paid no heed. I remember my small pile of possessions on the ground outside her truck as she drove away and the all-consuming grief that filled me as tears came flooding out. Now I understand the depth of my feelings was not just about my loss of Claire but also her leaving triggered issues of abandonment and loss of my mother as a child. In the years to come whenever I experienced the end of a relationship the same thing would happen and I would find myself experiencing what seemed to be unbearable pain disproportionate to the actual loss I was going through. My relationship with women has been heavily affected by my early experiences and it is only now after many years of hard work that I can say I have finally healed this deepest of my wounds.

With Claire gone it was time to live in my first bender. A bender is a small dwelling made from hazel poles that are stuck in the ground, bent over and tied to make a framework which then has a tarpaulin thrown over the whole structure. It is sturdier than a tent, and has the benefit that it is quite easy to install a wood burning stove inside for cooking and warmth. In my time on the road I lived in many benders and became more proficient at making them homely and comfortable. If you stayed in one place for long enough you could build a raised floor made out of pallets, cover them with carpets, line the walls with skins and blankets and install windows and shelves. There was something deeply satisfying about sleeping on my sheepskins against the earth, a connection with nature that we are far removed from living in houses made of brick. My first bender was not so comfortable. I had no wood burner at this stage and I would gather embers in an old frying pan from the communal open fire that we all lived around at night to take the chill off my home at bed time.

It sounds a bit uncomfortable and basic when I look back, and in some ways it was, but I now know I had to go through these times in order for me to be ripened by life. I needed time to grow and mature and I have no regrets for the time I spent living in this way on the road. In some ways it was what I wanted; to be close to nature, living simply and in other ways I was depriving myself of the need to take responsibility for anything. All I had to do was take one day at a time. But there was more, far more, for me to experience on the road before I was ready to move on to the next stage of my life. I hadn't hit rock bottom yet.

With the money that I earned planting trees I bought myself an old transit flat-bed truck from some gypsies. I left the site with my friend John and headed south a little way. It is often said that gypsies are not the best people to buy a used vehicle from and true to form the prop shaft fell off my vehicle a hundred miles or so down the road. I learnt this lesson quickly and have never bought another vehicle from such an unreliable source again. With no other choice, my friend and I put up our benders at the side of the road. I am not sure what the plan was, but we probably got stoned!

While shopping in Fort William one day we bumped into some other New Age Travellers. They offered to tow my broken down van to the site where they were parked up. It was a terrifying experience as the Land Rover towing me raced around small windy roads with me doing my best not to crash into the back of it. The new park-up was in a disused quarry and it was bleak. Being on the North side of the hill in winter-time meant it never got any sunshine. There was the usual pack of raggle-taggle dogs and an assortment of live-in vehicles but I soon realised these travellers were a little different from those I was used to. They were more a working class component of the traveller community. Their outlook on life seemed different to my previous travelling companions, they would drink copious amounts of Carlsberg Special Brew and there seemed to be a preference for harder drugs like speed rather than cannabis. The combination of speed and strong lager was lethal, and would often mean fights would break out, windows would be smashed and the night would ring out with sounds of anger, violence and chaos. It was a disconcerting place to be at first, but with a broken down vehicle and no money I was going nowhere fast. Faced with this reality, the old adage that says, 'if you can't beat them, join them', became true.

Whereas cannabis had numbed things a little for me, Special Brew and speed catapulted me into a whole new dimension of intoxication. It was not difficult to see the attraction as while you are under the influence you really do feel invincible and powerful. In those days it was a lot easier to claim unemployment benefits and we found other ways to make sure there frequently was money to be spent on drugs and alcohol. Shoplifting was rife. Supermarkets were the favoured targets and there was no real conscience involved in who was targeted. Small village shops were fair game and I even remember, to my embarrassment now, stealing from a charity shop once such was my lack of principles and values at the time. It was not uncommon for us to be banned from shops or to be chased out by shopkeepers with stolen goods falling out from under our coats. Money was for buying drugs; food could be accessed by other means. Waste skips were a rich source of supplementing our diets too. Missions under the cover of darkness to the back of the supermarket were common. We would jump into the skip and rifle through all the products that had been thrown out because they had reached their sell-by dates. It was rather exciting really as you never knew what you would find. Sometimes you would find delicacies and expensive produce whilst other times pickings would be minimal. Once the collector had chosen their bounty the rest would be distributed amongst fellow travellers back at the site. At times we would eat meat that was starting to change colour but by some miracle I never got food poisoning! In later days supermarkets got wise to our antics and they would lock skips away or pour bleach on the produce to make sure that it was not edible (even by our relaxed standards). It always struck me how wasteful our society is throwing away so much food when there were, and still are, many people in the world starving. It is a strange world we live in.

Another source of supplementing my diet was with the help of my dog. Almost everybody had a dog or two, and I was no exception. I spent many hours training my second dog, Rue, to be a hunter. Poaching became a passion and we ate plenty of rabbit, the odd pheasant and hare, and even the occasional deer. I loved the connection and teamwork with my dog and the additional thrill of being caught by gamekeepers only added to the experience.

By the time Rue died of natural causes I had moved into a house, but the death of my first dog was a little more dramatic. Her name was Bracken, and she was a beautiful gentle dog who, unfortunately, had a bit of a tendency to wander. At the time of her death I was parked up in Scotland, this time on the farm of an eccentric old German farmer. The farmer was happy for us to be there and there were quite a few of us, along with the chickens, dogs and goats. The farmers on adjoining farms were not so happy for us to be there, especially as there had in the past been incidents of dogs worrying and killing sheep. This was an on-going issue between travellers and farmers, and often it was down to the fact that travellers were irresponsible in the way they looked after their dogs. However, I am convinced to this day that Bracken never harmed any sheep, at least, she never returned from any of her wanderings with blood or wool around her white muzzle, which would have been the obvious clue. One day, Bracken returned from her wanderings with a bloody tail and it looked as if she had been peppered with shot from a gun. This was soon confirmed by an enraged farmer who arrived in our midst wielding his shotgun and demanding that he finish the dog off. He was angry and totally out of control and there were small children about. My friend Rob was the first to try and reason with him but the farmer was having none of it. He insisted that he would shoot the dog that had apparently been worrying his sheep. When the farmer refused to calm down my friend Rob made a sudden lunge for the shotgun in the farmer's hand in an attempt to pull it from him, but unfortunately the farmer had a better grip on it than Rob had anticipated. A brief game of tug-of-war took place, like something out of some bizarre comedy, with the shotgun being pulled first this way and then that. I was aware the shotgun was probably loaded and things were not looking good. Before I knew what I was doing I dived at the farmer and knocked him off balance which resulted in the shotgun now being in the hands of my friend Rob. It was one of those strange times when **conscious thought played no part in my actions, but my body seemed to make the decision of its own accord,**[4] and of course, it was one of those times that could have been the end of my journey through this life. The first thing Rob did was remove the cartridges from the gun, by this point the police had arrived and the farmer was led away. I don't think the farmer was charged for his actions - I do think the story may have been different if it had been one of us.

It seemed that Bracken was let off the hook and I did my best to keep her close by from then on but hated seeing her chained up all the time. On one occasion, when I let her off for a short while, she disappeared. It wasn't long before gun shots rang out down the valley and I prayed they had nothing to do with my dog. My prayers were in vain because a couple of hours later a police Land Rover pulled up. In the back was the bloody and lifeless body of my Bracken. I was charged by the police officer with owning a dog that had been worrying sheep and left with the body of my companion. I cried a lot that evening as I cuddled her lifeless body. Later I collected firewood to give her a fitting funeral, her body was burnt on a huge oak fire, and all that remained in the morning was ashes. Poor old Bracken. It felt as if she had been an innocent victim in the war between travellers and the rest of society. I was again reminded life can be tough and I had another emotional scar to bear.

This is not the end of this particular story - a few months later I was travelling in a van on the east coast of Scotland. A police car pulled us over to check the driver's documents and the policeman proceeded to ask for all of our names and dates of birth to radio through to the station. This was standard practice and I should have known better, but in the stoned haze that was my life I wasn't thinking too clearly and I proceeded to give him a false name. Unfortunately, I gave him the same false name that I had given to the policeman in relation to Bracken and the alleged sheep worrying incident a few months earlier. It was routine to give false names to the police as they had no way of checking our true identity. There were advantages to being of 'no fixed abode', however, there was, by this time, a warrant out for my arrest as I had not turned up to the court case, but travellers seldom did. Due to the length of time it took for a court case to be heard we knew we would be far down the road and the only way you might be caught was if you were daft enough to give the same dodgy name as the name on the warrant for your arrest! So I found myself in the back of a police car and spent the night in the cells before a brief hearing in court the following morning. I can't remember the outcome but needless to say next time I was stopped by the police I gave a different false name!

~

When I look back over those years, one of my favourite times was when a small group of us decided to move into a derelict village on a peninsula in The Highlands. It was off the beaten track and the only way to get there was a two mile walk over the hills or by boat. We built make-shift roofs onto the ruined crofts with our tarpaulins and with wood burning stoves installed they were a lovely space to live in. It was very peaceful. We would spend our days sitting around open fires, drinking tea and smoking dope. The water we drank was collected from the streams that trickled their way between our dwellings. Our work each day was to collect firewood and I became very skilled at tree surgery. There was an abundance of old oaks on the peninsula and these would be sawed and carried, sometimes long distances, on our shoulders to be cut into smaller pieces outside our dwellings. My bow saw became one of my best friends as it kept me fit and strong - it allowed me to get the wood to burn for warmth and the fuel to cook the food that nourished my body. Our diets were supplemented with shellfish from the sea shore, edible sea weed, and at that time there was also plenty of venison. Of course, we did not have permission to be there. It seems strange somebody owns every piece of land there is. The Native Americans have a different take on this and believe it is ridiculous to think we own any piece of land. Land is actually like our mother as it sustains us and provides everything we need to live. If anything it is the earth that owns us. I am inclined to agree.

I recall one day awakening to the calls of a policeman who had made the journey over the hills to remind us that we were camped illegally. At one point he was standing on an old fish box and he noticed that my dog, Rue, was sniffing around the box. He lifted the box to see what she was so interested in and to his surprise and my joy found nothing underneath. Fortunately for me I had moved a large lump of venison the day before that had been underneath the box. It was another of those times when, if things had been slightly different, I may have found myself in trouble but something or someone seemed to be looking out for me.

The worst thing about living on the peninsula were the midges. These relentless little insects did their best to feast on us and although a certain amount of immunity was developed to their bites it was often better to sit in the smoke from the fire than to endure their persistent and irritating acupuncture sessions. The weather too meant that life was sometimes challenging. The winter gales were fierce and it was not uncommon for nights to be spent getting up and down to replace huge rocks that were supposed to be holding the tarpaulin roofs down while the wind did its best to displace them. I remember one night after a fierce storm finding an injured puffin that had been blown in. I took it back to my croft and tried to nurse it back to health but it died. Nature's cycle of life and death was always very evident and in this remote and isolated place I learnt about her beauty and power. At night we lived by moonlight and candle light and some nights, silhouetted by the flickering flames of the fire, we were lucky enough to witness the splendour of the aurora borealis also known as the Northern Lights. As well as the adults there were half a dozen children with whom I shared my life at this time and their laughter and games brought an additional beauty to my days there. They were free souls and often played barefoot. They seemed happy enough making up their own games and getting into mischief. I wonder what they learnt from their time there and what affect it has had on them now they are grown up.

~

I can't remember clearly when or why I left the peninsula. I guess the restlessness within just had its way with me again, and it was time to move on. As well as restlessness, fear was a regular companion of mine and I see now it was an invaluable teacher and life on the road that helped me learn from fear, or rather how to face my fears. It is said there really are only two human emotions: love and fear. All 'positive' emotions are aspects of love, and all 'negative' emotions are aspects of fear. I see now you cannot have one without the other just as you cannot have day without night. **The experience of fear and darkness enables us to appreciate the light of love.**[5] We experience them both through contrast, and therefore the darker emotions are to be accepted and valued just as much as those that are easier and more pleasant to experience.

~

One day I learnt a valuable lesson about facing my fears. On a particular site where I was living there were a group of travellers who had known each other for a long time, and anyone who was not part of the 'tribe' was somehow seen as a threat, an outsider. Throughout my time on the road I was often aware that I didn't quite fit in and this was one of those times when this feeling of being the outsider was very apparent. Much of our time was spent sitting around open fires where we would cook and live communally. I became aware that, on more than one occasion, one man was giving me some rather unsavoury looks. He was a huge guy and had a reputation for being a fierce fighter. As time went by I became increasingly aware he did not like me and this made me feel increasingly uncomfortable and paranoid. One day, feeling that I could bare the discomfort no longer, I plucked up the courage to approach him while he was by himself and asked if I had done something to annoy him that I did not know about. To my surprise he became like a small boy and apologised telling me to take no notice of him and that he was being out of order. As you can imagine, I was very relieved by his response to my approach and from then on our relationship became much more amicable. This incident illustrated to me both the power of authentic communication and that **when we face our fears**

they often dissolve. Indeed, often overcoming our fears is actually the key to stepping into our own power.[6]

Fear can be a valuable ally and its purpose, fundamentally, seems to be to keep us safe but sometimes fears are also opportunities. They are gifts to be embraced and as we overcome them we become more aware of who we really are. I was to be reminded of this lesson many more times in the years to come and once by a rather unlikely teacher.

The teacher this time was a male pheasant! I stumbled upon him in a hedge while on a walk and in his fear and desperation to escape from me as I advanced he kept running into a wire mesh fence. Of course, this meant he was getting nowhere and after a short while he changed his tactics. By taking a few steps towards me (what he feared) he was able to get out of the hedge and fly away to freedom and safety. I was reminded of how often we waste our energy on strategies that are cleverly crafted so we do not need to face our fears. How much energy do we use in this way, when sometimes all we need to do is take steps towards facing our fears? Often the reality of confronting our fear is not as scary as we thought and when we take a step towards facing our fears the result is we feel a sense of liberation and pride in our achievements. The more we face our fears the more evidence we gather to encourage us to face new fears as they arise in our consciousness or in our lives. I endeavour to face my fears on a regular basis and although at times I fall prey to weakness and self-doubt, I know when I am ready I will take the steps necessary to overcome each new fear or challenge as it arises.

~

As time moved on, my lifestyle on the road began to take its toll upon my physical health. My diet was far from balanced, I rarely washed or brushed my teeth and I never went to the dentist or the doctors. There was nearly always somebody who had some knowledge of natural medicine and this was the usual course of action if you got ill. Along with the constant smoking and drug binges my body began to lose the battle to remain healthy. My teeth, or more specifically, my gums suffered most. At my worst, I would lie awake at night and it would feel as if my gums were on fire as they pulsed and throbbed in an alarming way. When I eventually began visiting a dentist, once I had moved into a house, it took a long time to get my gum disease under control. My gums are healthy now but I am reminded every time I brush my teeth by my receded gums of the lack of care for myself as a young man. I generally only owned the set of clothes that I wore and visits to launderettes at this time were few and far between. When my clothes became too smelly I would buy a new set from a charity shop and throw the dirty ones away. Once, when I finally got round to changing my clothes, I found they were riddled with body lice. It didn't really seem like a big deal at the time but it makes me shiver now when I think of it.

My skin became increasingly sore as my childhood eczema returned. I had suffered badly with eczema as a child and it faded when I reached adolescence as is often the case. Now it seemed my liver and kidneys could just not expel the toxins quickly enough from my body because of my steady diet of drugs and alcohol, and they seeped from my skin in a sore and itchy redness. I also suspect that the return of my eczema was due to the mounting pressure within to release the emotional pain from my childhood that still resided within me. I now know that when we have unexpressed emotions within us they often result in physical illness. A lack of ease, or dis-ease, is the root of many physical ailments. I know this is true, because later when I began to talk about my childhood for the first time, I initially became very ill and was covered in eczema from head to toe.

Sometimes things have to get worse before they get better! [7]
This was also the case with my life. Things had to get worse for me before I decided it was time I did something about my life in order to improve my situation. I sometimes feel that often we prevent people from taking responsibility for themselves and beginning their journey to wellness by doing too much for them. I call this 'the mattress syndrome' because instead of allowing people to fall and feel the pain of hitting the ground we throw mattresses under them to cushion the fall. In this way we prevent them from feeling the full impact of their choices and deprive them of the incentive to change their ways. There were no mattresses for me. I had little contact with my parents or family. I would ring occasionally when I had managed to secure a little casual work but for the most part I was ashamed of the mess I knew I was getting in and knew they didn't understand why I was living the way I was. Neither did I at the time. On the rare occasion I did go home my stepmother would put a blanket on the sofa before I was allowed to sit down. It was the sort of thing that you do for a dog to stop them making a mess of the furniture. It must have been hard for them and even harder for me.

~

The beginning of the end of my travelling days began one night when my friend and I had weighed in some whelks we had collected. Sea snail or whelk picking was a regular source of income. They were collected from the beaches at low tide to be sold to the local dealer who would export them to foreign lands where such delicacies were consumed. With our wages from selling our whelks we decided to walk the few miles to the nearest pub. The shops were closed and the pub was the only option available as we wanted to get drunk and the money was burning a hole in our pockets. Quite a few pints later we left the pub and, faced with the dreaded long walk home, my companion Darren decided that an alternative option would be to steal a vehicle. As it happened, the first vehicle we approached had the keys in the ignition. I feel totally ashamed of our actions now, but at the time I thought nothing of it. Finding the van had a full tank of diesel we decided to stop off and pick up our few belongings from the site and head south. I am not sure if we had a particular destination but I guess it seemed like a good idea at the time. With my friend driving we got as far as Edinburgh where we abandoned it and headed for a traveller site on the outskirts of the city. From the travellers on the site we heard that begging on the streets of Edinburgh was an easy way to make good money.

I soon discovered that this was true - all you had to do was sit on the floor, with a dog if you had one, and ask passers-by for any spare change. It seemed that I still had a little pride as I found it was much easier to do with a few beers inside me. I would stay in the city long enough to make sufficient money to buy enough drugs and alcohol for the night. The derelict caravan that was now our sleeping quarters had no fire or furnishings and hardly any windows. At the end of the day I would just stagger back to fall unconscious onto the floor, sometimes remembering to pull a thin blanket over me. The next morning would begin with consuming any leftover Special Brew from the night before while on the bus back into the city. For a few months this became my life. Sometimes we would end up gate-crashing people's parties we had heard about in the city, and other times we would frequent the Edinburgh pubs. The themes remained the same; begging, alcohol and drugs, followed at some point by an intoxicated unconsciousness. Life from the ground level of the street is an interesting perspective. Sometimes I was touched by the generosity of people and as Christmas drew nearer it was not uncommon to be able to beg forty or fifty pounds in an hour. You soon learned that the better dressed the people were, the less likely they were to give you anything, except for a look of scorn or pity, whereas little old ladies would often give what they could. Perhaps the fact I received so much from strangers on the streets of Edinburgh has helped inspire me to give more of myself now.

Now I know **when I give of myself I receive a great deal,**[8] but back then I was only interested in taking so that I could buy more beer to help me hide from the growing feeling of dis-ease inside me.

As time moved on, my companion, Darren became increasingly unpredictable. Even then I realised he was very messed up. His father had been in the army and was violent towards Darren when he was home. As a result Darren had a hatred of what he called 'squaddies' and would pick fights with anybody in military uniform whenever he could. He was an ex-football hooligan and had many tales of gang violence and atrocities inflicted on rival gangs. He sported a union jack and Swastika tattoo on his neck. He was not a big bloke but his apparent lack of fear made him intimidating. I had seen him floor men much bigger than himself with one punch. After a certain amount of drugs he would have a strange look in his eyes. As he stood there, facing me that night, with that axe raised above his head, I knew it was hit and miss whether I would be able to pacify him and remind him who I was. As luck would have it I did manage to talk him down. I think this incident was probably the straw that broke the camel's back and I knew I had to get away from Darren and my life on the streets as quickly as possible before I ended up being a casualty of his rage.

My escape plan was to head for Shaftsbury, where I knew some other travellers were living. I later heard that Darren was dead. He had choked on his own vomit after taking too much heroin. It was a sad end to what seemed to have been a pretty sad life. By this time heroin was rife in the traveller scene and overdoses were not uncommon amongst people I knew, along with the odd suicide or car crash. I knew I wanted out of the traveller scene, but the longer I travelled the harder it was to stop. I had no roots or anywhere to call home. The best I could do for now was to head south. I knew life as a single male was becoming increasingly less attractive and perhaps on one of the traveller sites of England I might find a woman who would rescue me from the chaos of the life I was living.

Lessons for Life

1. When the pain becomes too much or has been going on for too long it is often the factor that leads us to question our current situation, and it becomes a gift in the form of the catalyst to change.

2. When things happen to us as children we often interpret the events as being our fault; that we are somehow responsible for what happened. This is usually not the truth.

3. Challenges that arise in our lives are often opportunities to learn valuable lessons that help us to realise our full potential.

4. Our bodies have their own intelligence, and in times of emergency the body will sometimes take action before the mind has decided what to do.

5. The darkness of fear and other negative emotions enables us to experience and appreciate the light of love and other positive emotions.

6. When we face our fears they often dissolve. Indeed, often overcoming our fears is actually the key to stepping into our own power.

7. Sometimes things have to get worse before they get better.

8. The more you give the more you receive.

Chapter Three - Searching in the Dark

I wish that I could say that things got steadily better from here but, unfortunately, there was a little more chaos and pain to come. They say that chaos is needed to give birth to a star; just as the pain of childbirth brings forth new life there are times when **pain in our lives is sometimes the predecessor of something beautiful.**[1] That something beautiful was for me, my wife to be, Sally.

When I met Sally she had only recently split up from her boyfriend. It had been Sally's decision but James her boyfriend was not so keen on the idea. When I came onto the scene I became the target of his anger and grief. As was often the way in the traveller scene instead of sitting down and talking about things, alternative strategies of self-expression were employed.

I remember the night quite well. I was sat with some friends in my bender, on the edge of some woods, getting stoned as usual. Some dogs began to bark but I thought nothing of it as they would often bark at the slightest noise in the dark. My bender had an old car windscreen around the bottom of it as a makeshift window and the next thing that happened was an almighty crash as the glass from the shattered windscreen rained into the bender. Everybody promptly disappeared except for Sally and I who quickly realised it was James who had smashed the window and he was outside and he wasn't in a very good mood! He demanded I come out and face him like a man but when I peeked out I could see him stood by the doorway with a large iron bar raised above his head. Sally, incredibly bravely, decided to leave first in an attempt to pacify him but his response was to whack her around the legs with the iron bar as she emerged. Her cry prompted me to follow quickly after with the only thing I could find to vaguely defend myself with, which happened to be a cast iron frying pan! It was hardly the most intimidating of weapons but it didn't matter as it was promptly knocked from my grip by the iron bar, wrenching my wrist painfully. I made a dash through the darkness but in bare feet lost my footing in the slippery mud only to receive a painful blow across my back with the iron bar as I landed in the mud. Things were not looking good and I decided that my best option to survive this onslaught was to take refuge in one of my friends' vehicles. I would like to tell the tale of how I single-handedly disarmed him but I was no fighter at the best of times and with a sprained wrist and a very sore back I did not fancy my chances against this psychotic maniac. Regrettably, my friend was not keen on me staying in his vehicle too long as he was concerned it might get damaged.

James set about smashing up Sally's truck and when he was done with this began shouting at the top of his voice that I come out from wherever I was hiding. The point arrived when I realised I probably needed to get this over and done with and that things were probably not going to get better until he had had his pound of flesh. I nervously emerged from my friends' truck and everybody on the site gathered as I faced my enemy in the shadows. I was dismayed to find he towered quite a few inches above me and looked quite broad too. Why couldn't he have been a little chap?

To add further doubts to my wobbly confidence he was demanding we fight with knives. Needless to say, I told him knives were not an option and he reluctantly agreed, although I remember thinking as I strode towards him it was quite possible he had a knife on him, otherwise why would he have been into the idea in the first place? Hopeless fighter that I am I didn't even get one good punch in before we were tangled up in a mess wrestling in the mud. It reached one of those slow motion movie moments and I found that, to my alarm my hand and fingers were being pulled towards his mouth. As his teeth sunk through my soft flesh and into the top of my nail the excruciating pain caused me to let out an almighty yell. At the same time, to my embarrassment, my bowels decided to open too. I was experiencing first-hand the expression of 'shitting yourself'! As a result of my cry my friends intervened and they pulled us apart. I don't remember too much else. I was probably in shock. My friends did their best to clean up my torn and bloody finger which throbbed uncomfortably. I cleaned the rest of myself up as best I could. I seem to remember he paced around a little longer in the darkness but eventually got bored and drove off into the night.

The next morning Sally and I packed up what belongings we could into my old Ford Cortina and drove up to Scotland. The drive was painful with our injuries but we both knew we wanted to get as far as possible away from James and the memories of that horrible night. We headed for a small, quiet site where a few of my old friends were living in benders in some woods. Typically, the weather was foul when we arrived and I had to cut new hazel poles before I could construct our bender and move our belongings in and light a fire. At least we were safe and we were together. It was quite a start to our relationship and as we drove up the motorway I think we were both hoping it was worth it since we knew very little about each other or even whether we would get on.

Fortunately we did get on and our first son was conceived in the bender we built there under an ash tree. I have always struggled to define what it is to be in love, but I know that Sally and I grew together. We have since divorced and the story around that will be shared but we did spend fourteen years of our lives together and I can't speak for Sally but I have no regrets.

I remember phoning my parents to tell them I had met a beautiful woman and they would soon become grandparents. My stepmother was audibly shocked and did not hide the fact I seemed to have been acting quite irresponsibly. And when my dad came on the phone the only thing I can remember him saying was 'Is she educated?' Having fought hard for his education in later life education was understandably very important to him, but for me these were hardly the words that I wanted to hear.

~

Many years later when I was visited by my uncle I heard the words that I had been longing to hear. We spent a lovely day together and as my uncle left he turned and looked at me and said how proud he was of me. My eyes immediately filled with tears. I wanted my dad to be proud of me and to have said these words to me more than anything. He has since said these important words to me and I now know he is proud of me. I think that deep down all boys want to hear these words from their father. I have learnt this from personal experience and try to make a point regularly of telling my sons how proud I am of them. They don't need to achieve anything amazing; I am just proud that they are growing into beautiful young men and I am proud to have them as my sons.

~

In November of 1994 my son Ash was born. We named him Ash because as well as being conceived, he was also born under an Ash tree. We were living in a bender on a farm where I was working picking sprouts. Little did I know that this tiny baby would be the catalyst that would begin to transform my inner world and begin a whole new and very different chapter in my life.

The work on the farm where Ash was born was grim but it was work and it came with a park-up. A sprout farm is an unlikely place to give birth to a baby but it was our home at the time. Sally and I were intent on a home birth and the midwives were wonderfully supportive of our decision. It was not far to the nearest hospital if there had been complications. Ash was born late into a cold frosty night with the full moon shining down. It was an amazing experience and I am still incredibly proud of Sally's amazing courage and strength.

For the first year we stuck to terry nappies intent on not using disposable ones that were such a burden on the environment. This meant lots of hand washing and there was constantly a pan of soaking nappies on the wood burning stove. We wanted to bring Ash up as naturally as possible and chose not to give him traditional inoculations. Instead he was inoculated homoeopathically. He is sixteen now and although he was a colicky baby, resulting in being extremely hard work, he has always been very healthy and has never been seriously ill. I am sure this is largely due to his natural rearing.

~

After some time working on different farms in England, Sally and I returned to Scotland where we spent some time on the island of Lismore. A traveller friend of mine had bought an old croft on the island and was living in his bus with his young family while they renovated the croft. We moved over to the island to help him with the project. One job I had was to underpin the walls of the croft as it was built with no foundations. My task was to dig out two foot square sections of earth from under the walls and fill them with concrete. In this way the croft was strengthened with the addition of these foundations.

I later reflected on this work and saw it was a great metaphor for my life and the lives of many young people I have found myself working with. The point being, that as human beings, it would seem to be much simpler if we all began our lives with firm foundations. However, that is not always the way, and often we find early life experiences mean we are built on insecure foundations. The important point for me, which has given me great hope in my own journey of healing and my part in the journey of others is **we can underpin our own foundations long after we have reached adulthood,**[2] or to use the analogy of the croft, long after the roof has been put on.

John Bowlby's 'attachment theory' (a model related to human development and learning) states how our early relationship with our care-givers has a massive impact on our later relationships as adults and therefore the quality of our lives. **We all have human needs such as support, affection, safety and encouragement. If these are not adequately met as we grow up we find ourselves with a deficit which we are always trying to fill.**[3]

I attempted to fill my deficit by numbing myself with drugs which worked up to a point. When the drugs stopped working I had the option to choose stronger drugs. Fortunately, I did not choose this option and my approach since then has been to understand that the more consciously I meet my needs through positive relationships and in the way I live my life, the less my behaviour and emotions are dictated by old faulty programming from my childhood. In the same way that we can underpin the foundations of a croft after it has been built I continue to work on underpinning my own foundations. I am living proof that this approach works, as are many youngsters and adults that I have worked with.

~

The work on the croft came to an end and Sally and I made our way down to Herefordshire. While I worked Sally looked after our baby son and in the evenings we began to talk about doing something different. Sally and I were both disillusioned with the traveller scene but as often is the case in life, **although we knew what we did not want we were unclear as to what it was we did want.**[4] Some of our friends, also disillusioned with life on the road in Britain, had moved over to Europe and bought property that was very cheap at the time and were renovating it. We decided that we would do the same and began to save as much money as we could from the work we were doing on farms.

For a year or so we worked as much as we could and saved up to buy a vehicle that would take us to what we thought would be the 'promised land.' Sometimes Sally would work and I would look after our son and between us we picked beans, strawberries, raspberries and apples and also worked at harvesting hops. The pay was not great, but with very few overheads we were soon able to save up enough for the ferry crossing to Santander in Spain.

We bought an old Series 2 Land Rover and a beautiful 1960's Cheltenham caravan. The caravan had been semi gutted inside and I made some final alterations with my crude bow saw joinery. Just before we were due to leave the gear box packed up on the Land Rover and it was touch and go right up until the last minute whether it would be fixed in time for us to catch the ferry. In the end it was ready only hours before we were due to leave. We had decided we would head for Spain as we knew quite a few travellers who were living there and my Spanish, although rusty, would be good enough to get us by.

The plan was to make a new life for us; we both knew life on the road in Britain held little value for us anymore. It was at this time, travelling around Spain and Portugal, that I learnt one of life's biggest lessons: that **it does not really matter where you are because you are always with yourself.**[5] As the outer world is only a reflection of your inner world, even if you move location to what seems like paradise you will soon find that before long you will still feel the same. So often we try to change things on the outside to improve the quality of our lives, and although this may serve as a distraction for a while, if we do not change our beliefs and paradigms we soon find ourselves feeling dissatisfied and unhappy. Wherever we are becomes the right place to be when we are committed to our inner work and learn the lessons that life presents us in order to facilitate this process. '**We do not see the world as it is, we see the world as we are'. The amazing thing is that as we change for the better so does the world around us.**[6]

Sally and I did not know this at the time; we were looking for a new beginning and beyond this nothing else was clear. It was another necessary step on life's journey, which seems to me to be a bit like creating a carving from a block. The experiences I have had are like chiselling away at the wood. Every time I try something different and tread a new path, only to find that it is not quite what I want, I have removed a little more of the wood and am closer to revealing the finished sculpture. Unless we try different things how do we know what feels right and in alignment with the reason we are here on this earth? The more experiences I have, the closer I get to finish my sculpture. I imagine I will continue chiselling away at the sculpture of my life until I am an old man. I like to think I will perhaps have a little time near the end of this life to sit back and enjoy my creation.

~

Arriving in Spain with our Land Rover and caravan was quite scary. I was no mechanic, and although we had brought an array of spare parts with us, the fear of breaking down in a foreign country weighed heavily upon me. Fortunately, the Land Rover did not let us down and apart from leaving an oil trail (as is the way with old Land Rovers) all around Spain and Portugal there were no breakdowns. The old engine roared along, usually at about 40 miles an hour, as we made our way through northern Spain to Portugal and then down to the south of Spain. The cab was noisy and little Ash was terribly well-behaved considering the hours he spent strapped in his car seat. Sally certainly had her work cut out keeping him entertained for many hours while the landscapes around us gradually blended into each other.

It wasn't too long before we realised things in Europe were not much different to back home. We made our way from park-up to park-up, often congregating around settled traveller communities that lived in an array of self-renovated ruins. Although the landscape, geography and climate were different, people were still taking lots of drugs, sitting around drinking, playing music and doing various types of casual work. The only real difference was some people lived in houses rather than vehicles. I suppose I should have guessed as much. It was really just the same scene but in a different location. Some of the travellers were in Europe because they were wanted by the police for various crimes in Britain, others had emigrated to get away from the monotony of life on the road in Britain and the increasing amount of heroin addiction that was becoming rife. We found ourselves a long way from home, around pretty much the same sort of people, feeling worse than when we had set off, and the reality began to sink in, this was, by no stretch of the imagination, the 'promised land!'

We did have some interesting experiences in Spain and one place we visited made an impression on me. You could not drive there but instead had to make a half hour walk through the mountains near Malaga. Tucked away in a rather idyllic spot was a village of tepees. It was inhabited by travellers from all over the world and it occurs to me now it appealed to my desire to escape from the society I had grown up in. Barefoot children ran free and there was a calm and peaceful air about the place. We didn't stay long but the images of the place are still with me.

I did a bit of labouring while I was in Spain but was nearly always paid in cannabis and before long our money, as well as our enjoyment of the trip, began to waver. Slowly as the realisation dawned on us Spain was not what we had hoped it would be, we made the decision to start heading back to England and began to make our way back across Spain heading north.

We stopped for a while at my parent's place in Galicia where my now retired father was building a house with my stepmother. It was the most time I had spent around my parents since I had left home and it was quite apparent, despite our blood ties, we were strangers. It was quite a few years later before I began to build a relationship with my parents and I think at this time, unconsciously, I was still very angry about my experiences as a child and the lack of love I had received. I was living from a very unconscious place and it amazes me, to this day, I could live for so long with no awareness of the inner roads and paths that one needs to travel in search of inner peace, purpose and contentment.

~

Sally, Ash and I arrived back in England and the grey weather, as we got off the boat, was very much aligned with my mood. Now what? Although a little richer for the experience of completing the trip it seemed as if we were back in the same place. I was not aware of the metaphor of the uncarved block at this time and could not console myself with the knowledge that I was one step closer to finding out what I wanted. We headed for Herefordshire where we knew we could probably find a park-up and some work on a farm.

Some friends who were horse drawn travellers at this time were living outside Ledbury and they had been given permission by a kindly couple to camp in their woods; we joined them. After a while the grazing ran out for their horses and they were forced to move, but we stayed. I remain very grateful to these people for allowing us to live in their woods and they taught me not all people with money are to be distrusted. There was a general consensus on the road that rich people were to be despised as they had in some way 'sold out' to the values of society and the system, everything we were doing our best not to be a part of. The kindly couple were very caring and would sometimes invite us to their house for tea and cake. They were some of the first rich people I met who were kind and did not judge me and because of this I began to see **it is not always wise to judge a book by its cover.**[7]

I secured a steady job at a local organic vegetable farm and things on the outside seemed good. In those days a safe park-up and some work was considered to be nirvana! But inside all was not so good. My moods were becoming increasingly dark and the monotony of my existence weighed heavy upon me. There was a huge gaping hole within me; a restlessness and discontentment; a sense that something huge was not right. The drugs weren't working anymore. In fact cannabis had, for a long time, become a sleeping tablet and I would smoke pipe after pipe before I went to bed in order to get to sleep at night. There was no escaping the fact I was no longer able to numb the sense of unease that was within me.

Sally and I did our best to make some minor adjustments to the way we related to each other, to see if this would improve things, but they had little effect. I even stopped smoking for a month but this had little impact as I just drank more. In desperation one day I said that if things did not improve I would seek help from a counsellor. At least by this stage I knew I was the problem and was beginning to take some sort of responsibility. I never thought I would really go and see a counsellor - the thought was terrifying.

Time dragged on and I continued to be depressed and took much of my bad moods out on Sally; I know I was horrible to live with at that time. Perhaps the straw that broke the camel's back this time was when Sally decided to join a yoga class in Ledbury. It may seem like a pretty minor decision, but for me it was not. Massive amounts of insecurity arose in me and I now understand that Sally's decision to go to yoga was interpreted by the wounded little boy within me as the beginning of abandonment. I was terrified that Sally was moving on and the person that symbolised love and the feminine I had been so starved of as a child was going to leave me again. Poor Sally tried to reassure me and invited me to join her. I went once, but did not enjoy the experience, even though I saw no evidence of other men that she might run away with. Every week when yoga night would come round we would end up arguing as I attempted to unconsciously sabotage her growth and development for fear of losing her.

Her brother came to stay once too and I behaved appallingly. I became incredibly jealous and I remember the sound of her laughing with her brother sent me into an uncontrollable place of pain and torment. I understand now that **people often try to prevent others that they love from growing because of their own insecurities.**[8]   This is something I still have to deal with but my awareness and understanding of the situation makes things easier. I have since made a point of always encouraging my partner to fulfil their potential and spread their wings. Even though it still triggers a sense of insecurity within me the feeling is much less intense and I know that, one day soon, these feelings will no longer arise at all.

I was twenty seven by this time and Ash was two years old when things came to a head. I awoke one day with the stark realisation that my son would be better off being brought up without his father if things carried on as they did. I saw what a negative effect I was having on the family dynamics. I also realised that if I were to leave Sally and Ash it was very likely I would embark on a self-destructive drugs and alcohol trip. This had always been my coping mechanism up to this point and, with little incentive or understanding of how to stop this descent should I leave my family, I felt as if my back was against the wall and there was nowhere left to run.

But I still had one more chance. I had said I would see a counsellor if things between Sally and I did not resolve themselves and, true to my word, I set off one day for Hereford in search of help. A huge part of me was terrified, but the stakes were high and I had to at least give it a go. With no real plan, and not knowing really what I was doing, I found the MIND offices in Hereford and asked for some counselling. I was told I did not qualify as I did not have mental health issues - although I felt I could have argued quite convincingly to the contrary. I was directed to another organisation across the other side of the city, only to find they could not help me either. As I was leaving a man approached me and said he couldn't help but overhear what I had been saying. He told me he had been seeing a counsellor privately and he was happy to give me the counsellor's telephone number. It was again to be one of those pivotal moments in my life that appeared to have happened by chance. I wonder how things might have been different if I had not made contact with the counsellor I saw and where I might have ended up. Sometimes the precariousness of life and the massive importance of seemingly minor happenings and choices staggers me. I am reassured to have discovered there really are no *wrong* choices and perhaps we do not really make choices anyway. Perhaps something greater than us guides our choices and **whether we make rapid progress or find ourselves stuck in an uncomfortable place on our journey as a result of the choices, one experience is no less valuable than the other.**[9]

So there I was in Hereford, armed with a telephone number. This was before the days of mobile phones and I made my way to a public telephone box and made the call. An appointment was arranged and unbeknown to me I was about to embark on a whole new type of journey. My days of travelling in the physical sense in the world were at an end for now. The days of running away from myself had exhausted me; I had given it my best shot but no matter how far I had been and how fast I had run I had not managed to lose the shadow of my past. I had been to Israel and Turkey and Spain and Scotland in an attempt to avoid what lay within me. I had taken copious amounts of drugs and alcohol in an attempt to numb the dull ache I felt in my body, but none of it worked. It was time to begin something different where the landscape was totally unfamiliar to me; an uncharted landscape of shadows and greyness where ghosts of my past lay in wait. I couldn't really see how talking to a counsellor, somebody that was a stranger to me, was going to make things better and I was scared of the unknown, but I knew for the sake of my son and Sally, if not for my own sake, I had to at least try.

Lessons for Life

1. Pain in our lives has the potential to be the predecessor of something beautiful.

2. We can underpin our own foundations long after we have reached adulthood.

3. We all have human needs such as support, affection, safety and encouragement. If these are not adequately met as we grow up we find ourselves with a deficit which we are always trying to fill.

4. Often we know what we do not want but are unclear as to what it is that we do want.

5. It does not really matter where you are in the world because actually you are always with yourself.

6. 'We do not see the world as it is, we see the world as we are.' The amazing thing is that as we change for the better so does the world around us.

7. It is not always wise to judge a book by its cover.

8. People often try to prevent others that they love from growing because of their own insecurities.

9. Whether we make rapid progress or find ourselves stuck in an uncomfortable place on our journey as a result of the choices we make, one experience is no less valuable than the other.

Chapter Four - Making Changes

As a result of my experiences with the counsellor a whole load of new challenges began.

One of the first of these was that, after my second session, I became covered from head to toe with a very sore and itchy eczema outbreak. After the introductory session I spent the majority of time discussing and remembering my early childhood experiences. I was learning that **the mind and the body are interconnected and you cannot affect one without affecting the other.**[1] I began talking, for the first time, about my childhood and my body reacted severely. As I relived old experiences and the hidden feelings resurfaced the emotions manifested themselves physically as chronic eczema.

At this time my mind was not so open to allopathic medicine and I refused to see a doctor at first, or use any prescription creams that would have brought relief. The eczema had a massive impact on my self-confidence and I felt ugly and dirty all the time. Sleeping at night was sometimes difficult as the warmth of the duvet only caused the eczema to itch more. I spent some nights wandering on the Malvern Hills for the relief of the cool night air against my skin. Eventually though, as the homeopathy and acupuncture was not having a rapid enough affect and I was so uncomfortable in my skin, I made an appointment to see a doctor and started using hydrocortisone cream sparingly. It may be I had suffered more than I needed to because of ignorance and stubbornness but my thinking was still rather black and white. I was learning **it is best to have an open mind and not to 'throw the baby out with the bath water' as there is often wisdom in following a middle way**[2] that incorporates the better of two different approaches, whether it is in relation to health or something else. I was learning to be gentle with myself and I began to see my belief that holistic medicine was the only way, had led me to suffer more than I needed to.

I saw the counsellor about eight times and in this short period of time I underwent a massive paradigm shift. For the first time I saw I had been running away from myself, from my story, from what had happened to me, from who I was. I realised I had been cutting off my nose to spite my face and, to some degree; the years on the road were an attempt to live a life of self-neglect devoid of responsibility. I decided I had to change and was seeing there was an alternative to the downward spiral I had seemed to be trapped in for so long.

As a result of my therapy I saw I needed to make some significant changes to the way I was living. I stumbled across a very important principle which is: **for growth to take place there must be a balance of inner changes with positive action steps**[3] and with this in mind I saw there were three things I needed to do.

Firstly, I asked Sally if she would marry me. I wanted to show her I was committed to making it work between us and I was not just going to disappear when things got difficult. It was also a letting go of some of my traveller conditioning as getting married was looked on with scorn by many travellers as the kind of thing that 'straight' people did. I was turning my back on my travelling days as I was disappointed and disillusioned. It seemed to me, at the time, the years on the road had all largely been a waste of my life. I later realised this was not true.

Secondly, I realised I wanted to move into a house. I was sick of living in the restricted space of benders and caravans and, more importantly, I saw if I was to seriously embark on an inner journey of healing than I needed somewhere safe to do this. I needed to know I was not going to receive a knock on the door only to find a policeman there with another eviction notice. I wanted a home. Somewhere Sally, Ash and I could become a happy family. I went into town and found the council offices where I registered us as homeless and put our names down on the housing list with the hope of being offered a property.

Thirdly, I decided I wanted to get a job where I could work with people and perhaps begin to help other human beings in some way. My years of manual labour and 'donkey work' were over and it felt as if it was time to start accessing the caring qualities that lay within me. I began visiting the Job Centre and scouring the jobs sections of local papers in search of a new way of making a living.

These were the realisations that arose from my counselling sessions. I thought the counsellor was some sort of magician! One time I arrived for our meeting a little early and not expecting him to be about, I peered in through the window of the practice. He was sat completely still with his eyes closed. I later discovered that he was practising meditation in preparation for our meeting. This all seemed a bit weird to me at the time. Little did I know that I would soon become a meditator too as part of my inner journey and would be exposed to many other weird practices and concepts that would aid me in my transformation and healing.

As a result of my counselling I also decided I too wanted to become a counsellor. I was so moved by the whole experience, I decided I wanted to help others in the way this man had helped me. I didn't understand at the time how it all worked; all he seemed to do was ask a few questions and then sit back and listen while I would ramble on about this and that.

I now know he was introducing me to perhaps the most powerful skill that any helper of others must possess: the ability to listen deeply.

It never ceases to amaze me that **the quality of our listening has a profound effect on the person that is being heard.**[4] It seems when we are totally present with another human being we create the ideal conditions for learning and growth and change. Through deep listening we allow the wisdom that lies within the other to surface, giving the ability to see things differently and gain new insights into what is required in order to achieve whatever it is they want to achieve. The ability to listen is something I constantly aspire to improve. Sometimes we try to over-complicate things and although I know there is more to facilitating change in others than just listening, I never underestimate the power it has in the process.

My counsellor also inadvertently awoke in me the desire to learn again. I had sworn many years earlier I was done with learning from books and academic institutions, but I had not foreseen there may be things I wanted to learn about that I could not learn through experience alone. The fact I had been forced to spend years of my childhood in schools acquiring knowledge that I saw little value in had disillusioned me. All of a sudden I was faced with the prospect of learning something I could see was of value. I signed up for a one year qualification in counselling skills at Hereford College. My desire to learn and a thirst for knowledge had been awoken.

With our names on the housing list and classed as homeless with a young child we were soon offered a two bedroom flat in Colwall. It was a dump when we went to have a look and it didn't have an open fire - which seemed very important to us at the time - but we knew if we had refused it we would have gone to the bottom of the waiting list for a house. It didn't take too long to make it feel like home and our van and caravan were easily sold. It was wonderful to have so much space and it took a while to equip our new home as we had very few possessions while living on the road. It was a real treat to be able to flick a switch and have electric light and a gas fire without the long process of locating, transporting, sawing and burning firewood. Running water and the luxury of hot baths was also a real treat and, to this day, I do not take these things for granted.

Not long after we moved into the flat Sally and I were married at Ledbury registry office. It was a low key affair and I remember with some embarrassment that I was married in a suit that I rescued from a barn on the organic vegetable farm where I had been working! I had never owned a suit before and it seemed to be a waste of money to buy one, even from a charity shop, when the one from the barn happened to fit pretty well. Sally's parents and mine were the only people invited. Ironically, Ash had a plastic policeman's hat and he insisted on wearing it to the registry office! The brief ceremony was followed by a pub meal and that was that. We were married, we were living in a flat and all that remained was for me to get a job. It seemed in a short space of time we had 'sold out' and were living in a way, that for years, I had sworn I would never do. This was a stepping stone I had not expected to find myself on.

I stopped smoking cannabis pretty much straight away and, apart from the fact I didn't sleep too well to begin with, it was pretty easy. It wasn't fun being stoned anymore and I realised the thousands of pounds that had gone up in smoke over the years was probably enough - I had better things to spend my money on now.

I had no experience of working with people and no relevant qualifications but nevertheless it didn't take me long to get a job working with adults with severe learning disabilities in a residential home. It wasn't very pleasant work and seemed to involve a lot of dealing with human waste, but it was a start; I was working with people and for the first time it didn't really matter what the weather was doing - the years of working outside in the elements were over for me.

For the first year I worked part-time. I was still plagued with bad eczema as old emotions that I had suppressed for so long resurfaced and my energy levels were low. I felt like I was living in a grey bubble and now realise I was probably depressed. Sally and I both began to embark on a long list of alternative treatments to get us healthy after years of not looking after ourselves. I saw an acupuncturist, a homoeopath, a stress release therapist and had regular reflexology treatments from Sally.

I changed my diet, took supplements, started drinking lots of spring water, exercised regularly and began meditating. Fortunately, we had saved some money to pay for the complementary medicine when I had worked on the organic farm, but before long it was all gone. It was money well spent and gradually my skin began to heal as the complimentary therapies with the hydrocortisone cream worked their magic.

When we are young some of us don't tend to place very much emphasis on looking after our bodies but the truth is **our physical health has a massive impact on the quality of our lives.**[5] If I could turn back time I would have been a bit gentler with myself but I guess I didn't think I was worthy of really taking care of. Now I know differently.

We were settled into our new home and Ash began going to the playgroup in the village. It took quite a while to stop feeling like outsiders, as had always been the case while travelling, but we settled into village life. Sally progressed well with her qualification in reflexology, she had always been interested in complimentary therapies and, as well as being a self-taught herbalist, was a natural healer.

I was less threatened by her new passion to learn as I was busy with my counselling qualification. I still felt the odd one out in the classes and I would sometimes have anxiety attacks when I had to speak out in front of the group. I persevered. Every week when it was time to go there was a part of me that would try to sabotage the process and stop me from going. My self-esteem was still very low at this point and my eczema did not help at all. I was not used to being around 'normal' people and somehow felt I was a bit of a fraud and at any point I could be exposed as one. However, the tutor was very kind towards me and, if I am honest, I had a bit of a crush on her.

I found I would often become attracted to women who were kind and showed an interest in me. This was a clear throw-back to my attachment needs for love and affection and although Sally did her best she could never fill the huge gaping hole that still lay within me due to the eighteen years where most of my emotional needs were unmet. I later discovered I would have to learn to love myself before I could be reached by the love of another. This attraction to women and desire to meet needs that were not met in my childhood would sometimes lead to me taking steps that would eventually lead to the breakdown of my marriage.

The next key development for me was meeting a guy called Stuart. He worked at the same place as me and we became friends. As our friendship developed he began to tell me about a spiritual teacher that was holding talks and weekend retreats in the area. I struggled to get my head around the new concepts that Stu was introducing me to like consciousness and enlightenment and spiritual energy. When I told Sally about this spiritual teacher she was all ears and pretty soon she had made her mind up to go to a talk. I was more sceptical and found myself in a familiar place: I could either go along with her into something unknown that brought fear up in me; or I could leave her to it and deal with the fear that arose at the thought of her moving on, of her meeting someone more spiritual and abandoning me. Which fear was I to choose? Another seemingly small decision was made and I decided to go with her to the next workshop. I am an experiential learner by nature and I needed to check this spiritual teacher out.

The thing that struck me most about that day at the workshop was I felt surprisingly comfortable. The people there seemed to be very different, from all walks of life, but they all seemed very happy to accept me just as I was. I had never felt so at ease with a group of strangers in my life. I can't remember what the teacher Brendon said at all but there were lots of hugs and lots of sitting in pairs sharing the experiences of the various simple exercises and activities we did. Perhaps for the first time, through talking openly with others, I realised I was not alone. All these other people had their own fears and doubts and foibles and it was not just me. What a sense of relief!

When I left the workshop I was probably experiencing the first natural high feeling since I had left home. The sceptic in me was silenced. It didn't matter if it was all a load of rubbish or whether Brendon was a charlatan. I just knew I wanted more of this new feeling of warmth and softness, feeling at ease with others and within myself which I had experienced at the workshop. It was not long before Sally and I became regulars at Brendon's talks and retreats.

Another new feeling was the sense of achievement I felt when I successfully completed my BTEC counselling skills certificate. The course had been quite a journey for me - as much of it was very experiential there was lots of practice counselling with other members of the group. These sessions gave me an opportunity to express myself and I tentatively began to share little bits of myself and my story and, to my surprise, found that nobody was terribly shocked. Also during these practise sessions I began to realise, from feedback, I was naturally gifted with many of the core qualities of a counsellor.

I was particularly moved by the work of Carl Rogers and his three core conditions of empathy, congruence and unconditional positive regard. Rogers argued these three conditions were the keys to helping others. It seemed so simple but at the same time I realised to fully embody these qualities required a great deal of inner work, awareness and patience. To this day these qualities still make up the foundations of my work in enabling others.

As the course neared completion I felt less like the odd one out and felt hugely liberated to have shared with some a little of my closely guarded secret that I had only just left the lifestyle of a New Age Traveller. I had feared I would be judged in some way and the sense of shame and feeling that I had wasted many years of my life was eroded a little.

When I completed my counselling course the tutor suggested I do some voluntary work in order to keep practicing what I had learnt. There was no opportunity to practice my skills with the client group I was working with and developing my newly learnt skills seemed like a good idea. I was unsure of who to approach and how to go about securing a voluntary placement and my first step was to thumb through Yellow Pages. My thumb stopped at an organisation called the Youth Enquiry and Support Service (YESS) which had an office near to me. I had never really thought about working with young people before but for some reason I gave them a call and pretty soon I was hanging out with young people at their local drop in centre.

Again I am reminded of how **seemingly minor choices and actions we take have a significant part to play in how our lives unfold.**[6] If my thumb had stopped in a different place how would that have affected future developments in my life story? I suspect I would probably have ended up in a slightly different place but I would still have received many of the same challenges, gifts and opportunities that have helped me to cultivate my inner landscape. But I may be wrong; I guess I will never know for sure.

The lady who ran the YESS office was called Sarah and she was very motherly and friendly and made me feel welcomed. The young people were a little less welcoming and I was aware I felt a little awkward around them. I didn't get much opportunity to practice my counselling skills but as it turned out this was not the only reason why I was there.

After a month or so of volunteering Sarah asked if I would be interested in doing a Youth Work Qualification. As a volunteer there were no fees to pay. It seemed like a 'no brainer' and I was becoming more and more open to learning and realised that unless I wanted to work with adults with severe learning difficulties forever some more qualifications might come in handy. I accepted her offer and embarked on my second course of study.

Throughout the years that followed I found my proactive nature meant I was usually involved in some course of study or other. Sometimes the study was a traditional qualification, sometimes it was less traditional and often unrelated to the job I was doing. However, my learning would often become a significant factor in securing my next job. In this case the youth work qualification became my ticket out of the residential care home.

When I look back over my time at the care home there is one thing that stands out most. This is that most of the people who worked there had pretty low self-esteem too and many of them were attracted to the work because of the sense of power and control they had over the residents. The similarity between how staff and residents behaved was such that it was sometimes hard to know who the staff were and who the residents were.

I often felt the residents were treated with a lack of respect and dignity and it did not sit right with me - they were sometimes forced to do things they obviously did not want to do under the guise of encouraging them to lead an active, normal life. They were not 'normal' people and often they would become violent in an attempt to express their needs. I remember once sitting in a minibus next to a resident who was doing his utmost to bite and scratch me as we waited, for what seemed an inordinately long time, for some traffic lights to change so we could pull over and pacify him. He was terrified of going to the college to do woodwork, which he plainly had no interest in at all.

Most of the staff seemed oblivious to this and I suspect on some level it gave them a sense of power from their work and detracted from the fact they seemed to have little power or control over how their lives were at that particular point in time. This is a theme that would become evident too in the world of education and in many organisations I have worked where it often seems to be a case of the blind being led by others who have only slightly more vision.

~

At about this time I changed my name. My first name is Andrew and my middle name is Miguel. It felt like the right thing to do. I arrived one day at the care home and announced I wanted to be known as Miguel from this point on. Although my health and spirits were still not great I knew there was a great deal of change going on for me inside and the shedding of my old name was a way of letting go of the pain from the past and embracing the new Miguel that was slowly emerging. I also felt it was an acknowledgement and honouring of my Spanish mother who had chosen the name for me and perhaps marked the beginning of a process of loss and grief at her death. I was under no illusion that the changing of my name would not bring about a sudden miraculous healing and throughout this time my physical, mental and emotional health all improved at a frustratingly slow pace.

~

I know that my healing, although gradual, was accelerated by my time with Brendon. I will never know how much of it was about being directly in his presence and taking on board his teaching, or how much of it was due to being amongst a new type of people. Under Brendon's influence I became a seeker. I began to suspect there was more to life than meets the eye and I began asking some of the fundamental questions about the nature of life and death, reality, and who I was. I began to question what life was all about and whether perhaps we were more than just flesh and bones. Through my meditation I was forced to ask the ultimate question: who is it that is observing the dialogue of my mind?

I knew something was missing in my life and being around these people felt good. I began reading books about love and truth by spiritual teachers from around the world. My appetite for this new genre of knowledge was voracious and I read books by Osho, Barry Long, Ram Dass and many more. I was introduced to the Sufi mystics Hafiz and Rumi and found that deep within something was nourished by their words. They spoke of things that fascinated me and opened up a whole new hidden world of awareness and consciousness and mystery. I found solace and hope in their words as I was first introduced to the idea that **perhaps human suffering was a necessary prerequisite to growth and change.**[7] Perhaps everything was perfect and just as it was meant to be and perhaps there was a reason and benefit to be had from the suffering of my childhood.

I am under no illusion though that my introduction to Brendon may never have happened if it had not been for Sally. Although I enjoyed being around the other people that followed Brendon's teaching I didn't always feel totally comfortable around him. I always struggled with the way he was treated as an enlightened guru when he just seemed like a wise but normal man to me. If Sally had not been so devoted to attending his retreats and talks I probably would have fallen by the wayside much earlier and stopped listening to him but I was still very insecure and was fearful if I did not keep up I would get left behind. I guess in a strange way this fear led me forward. In this case fear pushed me away from something I was avoiding, in other words being without Sally, but the result was I was exposed to the teachings of Brendon that definitely awoke something deep within me.

I believe that I would probably not have got the job at Malvern Foyer if I had not been doing my Youth Work Qualification. I would not have been doing my youth work qualification if I had not paused my thumb at that precise point in Yellow Pages. My new friend Sarah at YESS told me about the part-time job vacancy and, encouraged by her, I submitted my application. I was pleasantly surprised to be offered the post and gladly accepted, knowing I had been ready for a while to leave the world of care work and clearing up human waste.

~

As my career began to unfold things were also changing at home. Ash was now at primary school and for the first time Sally was able to go to work. She had successfully completed her reflexology course and this had helped to improve her fragile self-esteem. Things in her home as a child had not been easy either and she had left school with few qualifications and was another casualty of a system intent on focusing on academic achievements. I was very pleased for her when she got a job as a teaching assistant in Ash's primary school as this was a big step in her development.

Things between us were ok but there was a distinct lack of passion in our relationship. In many areas Sally's needs were different from mine. This was partly down to our childhoods and partly down to the fact that she is a woman and I am a man. I am reminded, for example, of the adage: a woman needs to feel loved to have sex and a man needs to have sex to feel loved. This was very true for us and was not helped by the fact when Sally would ask me if I loved her I could not say 'yes'. I did not know if I loved her, as I did not know what love was. I always thought I would recognise love clearly when I encountered it, but I had no recollection of this experience.

This must have been very painful for her. I am now aware every relationship we have with the opposite sex is affected to some extent by our relationship to the same sex parent. Where did that leave me? With a dead mother and abusive stepmother it is not surprising my relationship with Sally was challenging. Much of my journey of transformation has been around my relationships with women and it has always felt as if it was my deepest wound. As a result of what happened as a child it seems I constructed a wall around my heart with the intention of not letting anybody in for fear they might leave me too. It seems this is what happened with Sally. I knew there was more to love than what I felt with Sally and instead of looking within myself and to my relationship with her for the answers my attention began to wander.

While on a weekend retreat with Brendon I became aware of a strong mutual attraction with a beautiful Scottish woman called Anna. Brendon's retreats led me into a strange place of inner stillness and sometimes waves of bliss would course through my body, while at other times it was not uncommon to find myself in floods of tears sometimes with the bliss and tears mingling. It was much the same as I had experienced years earlier while high on the drug ecstasy. In this altered state of consciousness it was beautiful to just sit and be with Anna. I don't think we even touched but we spoke of the feelings that were present in both of us. In my mind I had committed adultery for the first time since I had married Sally and though I felt it was wrong, it was a rare experience of feeling in my power as a man. I suppose that throughout all of my other encounters with women I had been numb with drugs. This was the first time I had experienced **the energy of attraction between a man and woman in a clear and conscious way. It was powerful and very beautiful.**[8] I wish I had felt this with Sally but the familiarity of living together and my inability to feel love seemed to have diminished the chances of this happening.

When I returned from the retreat I shared my experiences with Sally. I am not sure exactly what my motives were but I suspect they were a mixture of wanting to absolve myself of what felt like a sin and also a sense of duty to telling the truth. Maybe my motive was also to drive Sally away from me. Whatever my motive was the result was it began to create a distance between us that was hard to notice at first but over time became more apparent.

~

Meanwhile things at work were interesting - I had started working part-time at The Foyer (a residential home for homeless young adults). The part-time hours suited me well as my energy levels were still not 100% and, although I was no longer seeing any complimentary therapists, my recovery from years of self-neglect was not yet complete. Working at The Foyer was quite an initiation into working with youth. For some strange reason I thought I understood what it was they needed and much of it involved consistency, discipline and firm boundaries. While I now see these principles were important I totally overlooked their need for compassion and understanding and encouragement. I was, in effect, just giving them a dose of what I had received as a child and it took a while for me to soften up and realise they were in need of the qualities which I had lacked and still craved in my own life. Needless to say the young people let me know I wasn't meeting their needs and often gave me a really hard time.

Verbal abuse by groups of residents was quite common and I recall at times they would trick me and lock me out of my office or throw my possessions out of the window. It was quite humiliating and my ego took quite a bash. I was learning the hard way and my stubbornness and failure to see the obvious meant it was a while before I learnt about fully meeting the needs of others. Unfortunately, the managers did not seem to understand how to work best with these young people and there was little awareness or guidance from training or the other staff.

By this time I had grown my hair long again and was given the nickname of Jesus! On the walls of the residential home an artist had painted portraits of the staff and residents. It wasn't long before my portrait had been adjusted with a set of small devilish horns on my head! I was not terribly popular with many of the residents although with some I developed a good relationship. I admit I was arrogant and self-righteous and probably somewhat sanctimonious at times. These are some of the less attractive qualities I still possess but hopefully to a much lesser degree now. I am certainly grateful to particular young people who in their own way led me to see this.

I also struggled to build relationships with the staff at The Foyer but this was for different reasons. Most of them seemed to have trouble with clear and honest communication and in many cases it seemed as if the blind were again leading the blind. There seemed to be a mixture of reasons why people worked there, but the most common one that I could see was to meet their own needs. Staff were often very two-faced and would be very professional and reserved in staff meetings but it became obvious when they were alone with residents they would behave very differently. The key objective seemed to be becoming as popular with the residents as possible. Often this was best achieved by gossiping and putting down other members of staff. I did my best to stay out of this although I know I did not always succeed. It seemed to be the residents' favourite way of passing time and when I did not play the game it meant I would spend long shifts on my own with residents avoiding the staff room where I was based.

Night shifts were often eventful and it was not uncommon for an ambulance to be called out or back up staff to be called in to help sort out mini riots that were taking place. Frustrated by the inconsistency of staff and my role as enforcer of rules, that most were intent on defying, I became increasingly interested in the training and education side of the organisation. I began to see by doing too much for the young people we were depriving them of a sense of responsibility and disempowering them. Perhaps the solution lay in education and teaching them how to look after themselves. I was on the right track but soon realised there are many factors which need to be taken into consideration when considering education for disaffected youth.

One of the key issues for these young people was for the most part they were not 'ripe' for change and growth. Many had such negative experiences of learning from their time at school they immediately saw learning as a negative concept. They viewed learning as boring and their shortcomings in the world of academia only reinforced their low self-esteem and beliefs that they were stupid or thick. Also it seems to me most were not interested in improving their situation through their own efforts and were stuck in a victim mentality. It is no coincidence young people become homeless or disaffected and the factors that have led to this situation must be taken into consideration. **You cannot treat the symptoms effectively without first understanding and addressing the cause of the problem.**[9]

Most of the training on offer at The Foyer was an attempt to help residents secure employment; but most of the young people did not feel that they were worthy or capable of holding down a full-time job. Their primary focus was to have their immediate emotional and psychological needs met. This was the reason for their challenging behaviour as it was an unconscious way of communicating their needs. They were far from ready for the adult world of employment as most were like small children trapped inside adults bodies.

The other reason why the learning opportunities provided at the home seemed to be largely ineffectual was the teachers seemed to lack self-awareness and understanding of the young people's needs. It is essential a teacher sees the potential in their students and recognises that, although part of the job is to equip the young people with valuable skills, they will only engage with somebody they have a positive relationship with. In many ways this means the focus of the teacher is not so much about what they do with the young people - although varied and engaging sessions are important - but more important is who the teacher is; their levels of emotional literacy, their values and beliefs, their ability to build rapport and understand and meet the attachment needs of the young people. I was not aware of these important factors during this point in my career but I knew learning was the key to empowerment.

By now I had completed my youth work qualification. It had felt very much like a tick box exercise and I was not inspired by any of the tutors on the course but at least I had the qualification under my belt. It was not long before the next invitation to add a qualification to my curriculum vitae arose when I was asked by my employers if I wanted to do my City and Guilds 7407 qualification in adult learning. I readily agreed hoping this would equip me with the skills necessary to facilitate learning with the reluctant learners I found myself working with. Unfortunately, I was again somewhat disappointed with the content of the course, but I believe the qualification was key in securing my next job. My time at the residential home was becoming increasingly unrewarding, I was working full time now and as each shift approached I felt less and less inspired as the culture of the organisation seemed increasingly at odds with my own values and beliefs that were gradually becoming clearer to me.

But at last the mist began to clear and my next stepping stone became visible to me. It felt as if it was long overdue but I have since learnt that **life only allows us to move on when we have learnt all we can from the previous experience.**[10] I was aware I had much to learn about working with challenging young people. I knew most people in the sector seemed to have little understanding of the importance of meeting key emotional needs. I could also see that somehow learning was the key to growth and change. I was beginning to understand that life really is all about learning and that **quality of life is directly proportionate to the extent we are willing to learn and apply new found knowledge in our lives.**[11] As the mist settled the next stepping stone turned out to be a job in a college of further education.

Lessons for Life

1. The mind and the body are interconnected and you cannot affect one without affecting the other.

2. It is best to have an open mind and not to 'throw the baby out with the bath water' as there is often wisdom in following a middle way.

3. For growth there must be a balance of inner changes with positive action steps.

4. The quality of our listening has a profound effect on the person that is being heard.

5. Our physical health has a massive impact on the quality of our lives.

6. Seemingly minor choices and actions that we take have a significant part to play in how our lives unfold.

7. Perhaps human suffering is a necessary prerequisite to growth and change.

8. The energy of attraction between a man and woman in a clear and conscious way is powerful and very beautiful.

9. You cannot treat the symptoms effectively without first understanding and addressing the cause of the problem.

10. Life only allows us to move on when we have learnt all we can from the previous experience.

11. Quality of life is directly proportionate to the extent we are willing to learn and apply new found knowledge in our lives.

Chapter Five - Learning to Learn

As my journey within deepened I was drawn to attend a meditation course. I was struck by the presence of the guy who led the course. He would sit crossed-legged on the floor, almost motionless throughout the two hour sessions, while I would fidget and wriggle on my chair. He taught me different aspects and styles of meditation and the course was very illuminating. As well as meditation, I discovered that he taught Tai Chi and as the course drew to an end I asked if he would teach me. He responded in the negative and explained he only taught one person at a time and he already had a student. Somewhat disappointed I accepted his decision and forgot about Tai Chi...for now.

My spiritual teacher at this time was still Brendon. Sally and I continued to attend talks and retreats. Things had moved on though and Brendon's teachings began to focus more and more on the 'Divine Union' of masculine and feminine otherwise known as tantra. It has always felt to me there is more to the coming together of man and woman in sexual intimacy than merely just to procreate and tantra suggests that making love is another path to realisation of the Higher Self and enlightenment. Intuitively I felt there was something in this and with my need for physical intimacy and attraction to the feminine, I found that I was happy to entertain this belief. I was happy to explore this practice with Sally although the emotional baggage we were both carrying meant we never really made much progress.

It became common knowledge that Brendon was having sexual relationships with a number of different women at the same time. This is not uncommon amongst tantric masters but it was quite a challenge to accept without some degree of suspicion. I considered myself to be pretty open minded, but this pushed me further than I had been before. To this day I will never know whether he was abusing his position but I guess it is up to him and the women who he had relations with and is really none of my business. Nevertheless, I think my total acceptance of Brendon's teaching began to diminish and I began to see more and more that he was just a man and was fallible too.

Brendon's way of life challenged the notion I had always accepted that one man should be with one woman at a time and preferably for a lifetime. Through my reading around tantra, spirituality and religion the question arose whether conventional marriage was indeed natural to mankind or something that was imposed on us by religious leaders? Many different religions have different ideas about what is right or wrong when it comes to marriage. I have since come to the conclusion **there is no clear right or wrong and it is best to decide what feels right to me and allow others to do the same.**[1] I have since discovered that my personal preference is to have only one intimate partner in my life at a time. With my issues around relationships one is quite enough! I also feel it is not necessarily right for two people to stay together for life. I think as long as two people are nourishing each other and there is love between them then they should enjoy that time. The reason for being together is also to learn to understand ourselves more through the reflection of the other and this may bring challenge and pain too as we shed aspects of ourselves and our beliefs that are false and no longer serve us. However, it may be that the time arrives for things to change, people grow apart, the challenges may be too great and sometimes it is best for both to go their separate ways. Although partners may have travelled the road together and shared many beautiful experiences when the time is right it serves nobody to cling together through fear or obligation. **Some people we are meant to meet for a moment and others for a while longer and maybe some for a lifetime,**[2] it is up to each of us who we choose to share this life with and for how long. If we separate then it does not mean we have failed. I know from my experience of pain, separation and loss, these experiences will often lead to the birth of new things.

I recall a strange incident happening one time while I was on a retreat with Brendon. I had awoken in the night and made my way to toilet. I was stood relieving myself when I happened to notice something shiny out of the corner of my eye. I was wearing a t-shirt that had a mandala (sacred pattern) on it - the mandala was basically a lotus flower with some Sanskrit (ancient Indian language) symbols in the petals that spelled out a mantra. On bringing my attention to the t-shirt and the mandala I found it was the source of the shiny light that had caught my eye. As I looked more closely I saw a bright light whizzing around lighting up different colours of the mandala on my chest. In disbelief I rubbed my eyes and adjusted my focus believing it must have just been a figment of my imagination but to my amazement, however much I adjusted my focus, the light show continued. It was very strange but very beautiful too. Eventually I lost interest and just put it down to another one of those strange unexplained incidents that have peppered my life. My understanding of this, as with other hard to explain incidents, is **there is much more to life than that which we are able to perceive with our human senses and comprehend with the limitations of our minds.**[3] It seems totally feasible to me that if a dog can smell things we cannot and birds can follow a migration path with some sort of in-built radar system that I do not possess, then perhaps there is much more going on around us than our senses (or equipment) lead us to believe. The older I get the more evidence I acquire and the more I believe there is more to life than meets the eye. What if our understanding of reality and how things are is merely a little pond and beyond that what we can perceive with our senses is a vast ocean?

My time with Brendon also taught me about openness. In many of the satsangs (spiritual meetings) students would ask questions, Brendon would answer and discussions would ensue. Many of the questions were about deeply intimate subjects and gradually I learnt everybody had similar fears and issues and aspects they were ashamed of or needed to heal or just accept. There was great healing in the openness and trust at these times. It was liberating to reveal ones whole self and not be judged. So often we only present the aspect of ourselves that we are comfortable with or that we think others want to see. The more shadowy side remains hidden and can often fester and grow in the darkness of unconsciousness. My experience is **the more I reveal all of who I am, the more the shadows disappear and I become increasingly more at peace with myself.**[4] Among my friends who attended Brendon's workshops it was common practice to be demonstrative and share compliments and kind words freely. This was so liberating and I feel really is our natural state. Often human beings are so reserved and it felt lovely to be in such a mutually supportive space with people who were also committed to being the best they could be. I am reminded of a postcard I saw at Brendon's place that said: 'Be with those beings that honour your being.' I could see from my own experience this is the environment most conducive to our growth and as my life unfolds and I value myself more and more, I find myself surrounded by more and more beautiful people who nourish me, support my continued growth and in turn I do the same for them.

Eventually Brendon emigrated to New Zealand. He had been travelling the world more and more and when he left it seemed as if the time was right. I had learnt a great deal from the man and he had opened my mind to a whole new universe, but I was beginning to be my own guru and felt more and more that following the teachings of another was somehow giving away my own power. I am not interested in how he lived his life, who he slept with and what he did with them; that was up to him, just as my life is up to me. I am grateful for the many lessons I learnt through being around the man. By the time he left for New Zealand I was a very different man than the one who had sheepishly turned up at his workshop many years before.

Brendon is an example of how a person can have a big influence on our lives. I believe that **every encounter we have with every human being is an opportunity to improve the quality of their lives and in so doing improve the quality of our own**.[5] This may involve a small thing like a smile or a 'hello' to a stranger passing by. It could be giving way to another motorist, or helping somebody with a heavy bag. Or it could be giving somebody a compliment. It is easy to enrich the lives of others. If everybody thought in this way the world would be an even more wonderful place to live. Other people stay in our lives for considerably longer and this means we have the opportunity to have even more of a positive difference. But no matter whether the encounter is brief or lasts many years, no positive thought or action should ever be underestimated. Something that is small to us may be something of great importance to someone else.

The next mentor who came into my life was another interesting man. His name was Pete, he was an unusual character and I learnt an awful lot from him too. He was completely different to Brendon and his teachings were not of the inner landscape but of the world of education and business.

I first met him at my interview for the post of learning supervisor at the college. He asked me to balance 20 six-inch nails on one nail which was stood upright in a block of wood. I did not know how to do it at the time and after a few attempts I had to give up. I later discovered it was Pete's way of seeing how I dealt with a problem I was unlikely to be able to solve. I do not remember exactly what I felt at the time but I know I laughed quite a lot! Pete later showed me how to solve the problem and this unusual approach to job interviews was a valuable insight into the man who would become a good friend and my mentor while at the college.

On the first day of my new job I arrived punctually only to find there was no sign of Pete who I was to be working with. Nobody seemed to know where he was. I sat uncomfortably in a small office and waited for what seemed an eternity. Eventually he arrived in shorts and t-shirt, sweaty and red faced. I discovered Pete cycled into work and on this occasion he had had a puncture. It was a funny start to what I viewed at the time as my introduction to a slick organisation about to teach me all I needed to know in order to begin my career and become a successful teacher. I soon realised Pete was a bit of a maverick and his unconventional approach to learning and organisations was just what I needed.

Pete told me of how, in the previous year, he had designed and delivered a course for disaffected young adults and the result was this had an adverse effect on his health and his sanity! My role was to ease the burden, bring new ideas and begin team teaching the new group of students that had enrolled on the course. Paul seemed to be a very competent teacher, had the help of a teaching assistant Sandra, and there were only seven students in the group. I couldn't help but wonder how such a small group of students could have such an impact and necessitate the decision to add another member of staff to the team. When the boys arrived I began to understand!

Fortunately, under the guidance of Pete, I learned quickly on the job. The course was designed to equip the students with some basic qualifications and give them a positive experience of learning. Most of them were from Year 10 of a local secondary school where they had been causing all sorts of problems when they bothered to turn up. They would come to college for three days each week and attend our course. The first day would begin with a journal session and this allowed them to share tales of adventures they had had over the weekend. These adventures usually involved 'run-ins' with authority and drug taking with a bit of music and football thrown in for good measure. I quickly saw I had had quite a lot in common with these boys and, while I had lived my wild days on traveller sites, they were living their wild times on the rougher estates of the city and had started their exploration of drugs much earlier than I had.

After the journal session we would have a sports session in an attempt to get rid of some excess energy. We were supposed to try lots of different sports with them but they strongly favoured football and we played a lot of this. Most of them were actually very good footballers and could have played for local teams if they had learnt to handle their emotions. The sports sessions were very competitive with vast amounts of testosterone flying about all over the place. Fortunately, despite the enthusiasm and energy of the boys, I only suffered one cracked rib due to a rather over-exuberant tackle.

Apart from the sports sessions, we also took the boys each Thursday to a working farm to use up some energy. Here they would learn practical skills like constructing bird boxes and benches or building brick barbecues. The week ended with a self-assessment session where the boys would take it in turns to assess themselves based on their behaviour and achievements through the week. They were surprisingly good at this and quickly showed they were fully aware of when they were doing their best and when they were not. The rest of the time was filled with sessions Pete and I designed or adapted to encourage them to solve problems, work together and communicate effectively. It was hard work - but it was worth it as these boys and the groups I worked with in the coming years at the college taught me much about learning and education. I know I learnt much more from them than they did from me. It was a tough initiation but I now see that by working out gradually how to engage these reluctant learners I learnt the key components that create the ideal conditions for learning to take place.

My initial thoughts while working in the homeless sector were largely confirmed and I saw the relationship with the learners was massively important. Pete was a big guy and although he had a good sense of humour he was able to impose order and obedience much better than I could. I was nervous around the boys at the beginning and they picked up on this. Over time my confidence grew and as the years passed at the college I became more competent as a facilitator of learning. I began to focus more and more on meeting their emotional needs and this meant rapport grew and with this their behaviour and learning improved too.

I adopted many aspects of Pete's laid back way of teaching; other aspects I decided were not for me and over time I developed my own style. I suppose my style was directly related to my values and principles that were becoming clearer and of more importance to me as I began to rediscover who I was. The key values that were emerging were authenticity, integrity, honesty, love and respect. These values were like a guiding light that shaped the way I taught and the man that I was becoming.

Pete was also a valuable mentor in relation to being within an organisation. He knew his own mind and if he was asked to do something that he did not feel was right he would not do it; he was always professional about it but firm. I heard many staff around me moaning about other staff or managers and I could not understand why they did not do something about the things they were unhappy with. Most of them had been there so long they seemed to have lost their enthusiasm and belief in their work. Pete was not like this and I appreciated his attitude. During lunchtimes Pete and I would walk by the river. I learnt the value of taking time out and relaxing and noticed many of our best sessions were created and the toughest problems were solved while walking and talking in this natural atmosphere.

Pete also had a mild contempt for authority within the college - just because someone was his boss did not mean that Pete respected them. There were few people Pete seemed to respect at the college and it was a pretty safe bet those he did respect were worth knowing. Under Pete's guidance I learnt to make up my own opinion about someone's contribution and value rather than assuming their position defined who they were.

One day I was stood at the college in a small queue, waiting to use the photocopier. Pete was with me and I was talking in quite an animated way to him about the lesson we were about to deliver. A lecturer in the queue turned round and looked at Pete and said 'blimey he hasn't been here long has he?' It was assumed my enthusiasm would fade over time and I would be run down and discontented as many of the lecturers seemed to be. I made a vow to myself that day, if I ever became disgruntled and disillusioned at the college then I would leave. I would not remain somewhere doing a job I did not believe in. I firmly believe **life is too short for spending too long doing things that do not nourish us.**[6]

Pete retired and left the college a couple of years before it was my time to leave. I missed his companionship and wisdom a great deal. We had become good friends but I feel I had learned all I could from Pete and it was time for our paths to part. It was time for me to put into practice what I had learnt from him and continue my journey as a teacher by myself.

The day did come when I became increasingly disillusioned by what I saw at the college. The qualifications and awareness of staff meant a focus on suppressing symptoms instead of focusing on fundamental self-esteem and attachment issues, while the fearful and damaged young people were screaming out 'meet my needs, please help me strengthen my inadequate foundations.' The time would come when I could begin to work in a way that was more in alignment with my understanding and beliefs but I still had a lot more to learn from the young people I worked with at the college before it was time for me to leave.

~

At home things were okay. Ash had settled in well to primary school and Sally became pregnant with our second son. He was named Sol by way of acknowledgement of my Spanish blood and mother and also because he was born in the middle of the summer.   Sally opted for a home birth and again the midwives were supportive of this.   It was another proud moment for me especially as only Sally and I were present when Sol was born because the midwife arrived a little late!

A curious thing happened the morning Sol was born, which I remember clearly. I am not sure I believe in coincidences and prefer to believe that everything happens for a reason. Sometimes it is difficult to understand why or how things happen but often, after the passing of time, we can see if one thing had not happened a whole chain of events may have been affected. **Sometimes things, which at first glance seem unimportant, become crucial to the way our lives unfold**[7] and so I have learnt to be aware and mindful of such incidents.

When Sally's waters broke first thing in the morning I decided it would be a good idea to take Rue, our dog, out for a quick walk before all the action started happening. In a field behind the house where I took Rue there was a horse tethered. Sadly it had got the rope tangled around its back leg and was obviously in some distress. I came to its assistance and untangled the rope. On my return home Sally was already full into the labour and a little concerned that no midwives had arrived. I did my best to reassure Sally we would be fine without the midwives and she was incredibly brave and calm about the whole situation. Things happened quickly and by the time she was in her chosen birthing position on all fours in the living room Sol's head was already showing. After a few pushes and some swear words, out he popped into my waiting hands. Interestingly the umbilical cord was wrapped around his leg and having practiced this manoeuvre earlier with the horse, I remained calm. I was just working out how to untangle the chord without dropping my slippery treasure when the midwife appeared at the door.

Now it seemed a bit odd to me I should have two encounters with tangled ropes and legs on the same morning. It may be it was just coincidence but I like to believe the incident with the horse was a 'practice run' and meant when I saw Sol's tangle I remained calm and therefore did not transfer any stress onto Sally or my newborn son. Sally and Sol were both healthy and it was another amazing experience that I shall never forget.

The new addition to our family was beautiful, he also suffered from colic and was hard work, particularly for Sally, as she was in charge of the night shift.   It was a strange time for me because just as with the birth of Ash the birth of Sol meant that, although I was a proud father, on some level I grieved the loss of my woman. Sally was tired and much of her time and energy was spent looking after our newborn and his brother. With my insecurities I found it difficult. It was just the way it was and like many men that lose their connection with their wives at this time I found I began to increasingly divert my energy elsewhere.   Having a strong need for intimacy and feminine attention I stumbled across what seemed like the perfect solution in the form of Biodanza.

Biodanza is a system of human integration and growth, stimulated by music, rhythm and emotion. It aims to promote personal development and a richer enjoyment of life through creative dance to various pieces of music; sometimes alone, sometimes in groups and sometimes in pairs. I joined a Biodanza group and quickly fell in love with my fortnightly sessions. I did not fully realise it at the time but it nourished my need for intimacy, closeness, self- expression and most importantly female attention! I loved the thrill of being able to dance very intimately with a beautiful woman who I was not familiar with. The mystery and the unknown are great vehicles for promoting passion and intrigue! It was all done in a very safe and respectful way and I learnt to read sensitive aspects of body language that would indicate how close a woman wanted to get. I am under no illusion it was a substitute for the lack of passion that existed between Sally and me and on some level she knew this too. A woman's intuition is never to be underestimated!

There was more to Biodanza than just the expression and exploration of sexual energy though - I learnt about deepening my connection with other human beings as I had also done with Brendon, but in a different way. As well as enjoying dance and movement with women that I was attracted to, I enjoyed sharing the dance with other men and other women of which there was no physical attraction at all. I came to see and appreciate the beauty and humanness of other beings as we shared in the rich variety of emotions that were allowed to be expressed in the dance. My childhood had been so starved of closeness and affection I saw Biodanza as a way of meeting my needs in a beautiful and respectful way. I know that as my needs were met I also met the needs of my fellow dancers in the exchange of openness and compassion for each other.

Understandably these were difficult times for Sally. I would sometimes return from a class in a state of bliss and although she was glad I was enjoying my dancing she also knew much of my enjoyment came from being with other women. In my desperate desire to have my needs met I overlooked her needs. We continued to have sex regularly and sometimes it was very beautiful but as I look back I see that for Sally it became more a sense of obligation. For me it was increasingly a desperate attempt to reconnect with her while all the time, on some deeper level, she was closing herself to me knowing that in my mind I was making love to other women. I had lost Sally's trust and this would never return. We never shouted or became aggressive but more and more frequently we would find ourselves talking together about the distance that was becoming difficult to ignore. I did my best to appease Sally's feelings and felt sure we were making progress and when I stopped going to Biodanza I hoped my thoughts and feelings around other women would stop.

However, I had discovered some women found me attractive and, like a magnet, was drawn to receive the attention that came my way. I became quite a flirt, usually when Sally was not about but under the influence of alcohol I occasionally flirted while Sally was present, almost oblivious to her and the pain I was causing. Eventually Sally would decide that enough was enough, but we both felt that to separate would mean we had failed and we were both fearful of what that might mean for our boys as well as ourselves. We agreed we would not give in and would continue to try and make our marriage work.

Some people seem to find something that nourishes them and they stick to it. It may be a sport or dance or painting or making music, but I have always found that like a bumble bee taking pollen from different flowers I like to explore different paths to learning, growth and self development. The attraction of Biodanza became less when the teacher emigrated and was replaced by another woman. I am aware that often my connection and respect for the person leading workshops I attend is as important as the subject that they are teaching. I have been to too many seminars and workshops in my time and the ones in which I have learnt most were always those where I felt the teacher was a person of integrity and authenticity and that they obviously practiced what they preached. My new Biodanza teacher seemed false and conceited and before long I had stopped going.

The end of dancing meant I was hungry for a new discipline to help me stay fit and nourish me. With this in mind I got back in touch with my old meditation teacher and asked him again if he would teach me Tai Chi. My persistence paid off and it just so happened he had recently finished teaching his latest Tai Chi student. He seemed to agree reluctantly and tested my commitment by informing me Tai Chi was probably the most difficult thing I would ever learn. I thought little of this comment at the time and assured him I would be at his house the following Tuesday and would be ready to begin.

I see that sometimes my ignorance and arrogance have been a blessing as there have been a few things in my life I would probably never have begun if I had known how difficult they would be. Fortunately my stubbornness and resilience have helped me out in these situations and when I embark on something I rarely give up until I have accomplished what I have set out to do. Learning Tai Chi pushed me to my limits and my new Tai Chi teacher was not wrong when he had warned it would not be easy.

It took me a year and a half of one hour lessons, once a week and practicing daily, to master the Yang style Tai Chi short form, which in its entirety is only about five minutes long.

Every lesson would begin with warm up exercises to strengthen my legs as leg strength is essential to being able to do Tai Chi. Although a physical practice I soon became aware that to learn Tai Chi I would also have to make great advances in mastering my mind. My teacher was no fool and being also a master of meditation he knew more about my mind than I did!

I discovered it is very difficult to coordinate both arms doing something different at the same time as both legs were also doing something different. My mind began to protest and feelings of inadequacy and stupidity became my constant companions during the lessons. Every part of my being was soon screaming 'give this up, you're never going to get the hang of this.' My teacher seemed to move so effortlessly through the postures while I would feel like a totally uncoordinated reprobate! Juan my teacher was quite happy to point this out to me at regular intervals and his taunts would result in laughter and ease the tension that was often building in my mind.

The worst point of each lesson would come when Juan would say 'right let's move on to the next bit.' I would already be struggling with the posture I was on and my poor mind would protest. Interestingly, what I discovered every week was when the new bit of the form was introduced the previous bit, that had seemed so difficult, would fall into place. My teacher knew this and was in effect tricking my mind. With a whole new problem to get in a fluster about my mind would relax about the part of the form I had just begun to learn and the movements would somehow become easier.

This experience was a powerful lesson to me and throughout my life I see how **the mind likes to focus on the current biggest problem it can find.**[8] While focusing on a problem the result is I become emotional and in this state it is difficult to see clearly and resolve the problem. However, once I shift my mind's focus onto something else the problem usually becomes less of a problem and often resolves itself. The trick is then to remain mindful as the tendency for my mind is to quickly find something else to worry about. I suppose it is just my minds way of drawing my attention to aspects it feels need attention and it means well!

As time passed Juan and I became good friends. We would often share a whisky after our physical exercise as Juan was rather partial to his single malt. We would talk and Juan would often shed light on current issues in my life. I was beginning to think about becoming self- employed and was talking about this with Juan. He suggested I get some articles published to raise my profile. I assumed he was talking about some publicity in a local paper but he corrected me saying I should set my sights higher on a publication like the Times Educational Supplement (TES). This seemed a bit unrealistic to me and my initial thought was 'little old me' could never get an article published in such a reputable magazine.

Nevertheless, Juan had sown a seed in my mind as is the way with good teachers and gradually over time the idea of writing an article and sending it to the Times seemed less and less unrealistic. It was not until a few weeks later though that a chance encounter confirmed to me that writing an article for The Times was what I needed to do. It was another one of those times when I was forced to consider there is a higher guiding force active within our lives; something beyond comprehension of the mind and something that can only really be experienced directly.

On this particular day, I had been delivering some training in London. I returned to Paddington train station and had found a couple of empty seats on the train. I sat by the window and began to read my book. Just before the train pulled away from the station a lady came and sat beside me. She was dressed smartly, looked professional and I remember her perfume smelt lovely. I greeted her politely as she arranged herself in the seat next to me and I continued to read my book. Out of the corner of my eye I noticed her take out a magazine from her bag which she began to browse through. Although I could not make out the words, the colours of the cover caught my eye and by way of making conversation I asked her what she was reading. She replied it was the Times Educational Supplement to which I was somewhat surprised as this was the second time this previously unheard of publication had come up in a few days. We exchanged a little polite conversation and she returned to her reading and I to mine. In truth I struggled to focus on my book and instead thoughts of writing an article filled my mind.

After a while the train came to a stop at a station and the lady beside me got up to leave. I turned to face her and we exchanged goodbyes. As she left she reached into her bag and handed me the magazine saying: 'You can have this one if you like. It's rather a good read. I should know, I am the editor.' I was too shocked to be able to say anything coherent and she disappeared down the aisle of the train. I was left sitting with the TES magazine in my hand and a strange sense that a miracle of some sort had just taken place. I guess it could have been another coincidence but what were the chances I would be on *that* train, at *that* exact time and place to find myself sat next to the editor of the Times Educational Supplement?

On arriving home I went on to the internet and looked up the editor of the TES. There was a photo of the lady who had sat next to me on the train on the website and, sure enough, she was who she said she was. I sent her an email telling her briefly of the significance of our meeting and enquired as to who I should send my article to; definitely realising I now had to write it. She sent me the details I asked for and wished me well. The very next day I emailed my first draft; it was not accepted. It took three attempts and many hours to get it right, but finally I received the email thanking me, saying they would let me know which publication my article would appear in.

I learnt a lot from this experience. Perhaps, most importantly, I was reminded again there is more to life than meets the eye. I also learnt I was no less than anyone else and when I put my mind to something I could achieve my objective. I experienced a massive boost in my self-belief in relation to my possible achievements and learnt it is a good idea to talk to the person next to you on the train!

~

Three years on I had finally learnt the movements of the Tai Chi form and the mirror form, and though I am fully aware the learning and deepening of Tai Chi never really stops, it meant I now had a framework of flowing movement to practice. Tai Chi is a moving meditation and it is perfected when the mind the breath and the body are all in total alignment. This is similar to how I experience my life and I see **the more my beliefs, thoughts and actions are all fully in alignment the more alive and at peace I feel.**[9]

Tai Chi is in itself a metaphor for life and has taught me to use my energy wisely - as a martial art it draws on the energy of the opponent and enables us to use it to overcome their attacks. I have chosen what at first seemed to be my enemies, my challenges and wounds, and used them as tools and lessons for my own healing and growth. Although graceful in appearance, Tai Chi is also known as the dance of silk around steel and is a very effective form of self-defence. In the same way I do my best to flow and be kind and yielding at my centre there is increasingly a sense of strength. Ones power in Tai Chi comes not from tension and force but from yielding and flow just as water in its fluidity is also tremendously powerful. There are many things I have gained from learning Tai Chi but perhaps the most important is **great things can be achieved if we take things one step at a time, practice diligently and refuse to give up.**[10]

I still practice my Tai Chi for half an hour at the start of most days. It centres me and is a way of honouring this body I have been blessed with and which I abused for so many years. It keeps me strong and supple and also does the same for my mind as Tai Chi helps the integration of both the right and left hemispheres of the brain. I have not taught anybody else Tai Chi yet, but I know the time will come soon when this opportunity will arise. This will be most welcome and will further deepen my understanding and competence at Tai Chi. It is very true that **in order to learn effectively we must first be taught the knowledge and skills, then we need to apply what we have been taught and lastly we must teach others.**[11] I believe this last step of teaching others is the true test of whether we have truly learnt something.

This period of my life was one in which I was graced by the support and wisdom of two great men. In very different ways Pete and Juan both played a massive part in my life and the shaping of my character. My father gave me very little guidance on how to be a man in the world and these men were, in a way, surrogate fathers. I am honoured they gave so much time and energy to me and I now know this was partly because they could see a potential in me I was not yet ready to see myself. In their belief in me they played a tremendous part in my ability to begin to believe in myself. Such is the way; **when we believe in another it is only a matter of time before they begin to believe in themselves.**[12] As my self-belief began to grow, so things in my life continued to change too.

Lessons for Life

1. There is often no clear right or wrong and it is best to decide what feels right to me and allow others to do the same.

2. Some people we are meant to meet for a moment and others for a while longer and maybe some for a lifetime.

3. There is much more to life than that which we are able to perceive with our human senses and comprehend with the limitations of our minds.

4. The more I reveal all of who I am the more the shadows disappear and I become increasingly more at peace with myself.

5. Every encounter we have with every human being is an opportunity to improve the quality of their lives and in so doing improve the quality of our own.

6. Life is too short for spending too long doing things that do not nourish us.

7. Sometimes things which at first glance seem unimportant become crucial to the way our lives unfold.

8. The mind likes to focus on the current biggest problem it can find.

9. The more my beliefs, thoughts and actions are all fully in alignment the more alive and at peace I feel.

10. Great things can be achieved if we take things one step at a time, practise diligently and refuse to give up.

11. In order to learn effectively we must first be taught the knowledge and skills, then we need to apply what we have been taught and lastly we must teach others.

12. When we believe in another it is only a matter of time before they begin to believe in themselves.

Chapter Six – Wounded

As I look back I can see so clearly everything that happened on my journey was necessary. Every encounter with every person, every choice I made and every step I took has resulted in me being here and now. There is so much peace in knowing this for me, as I see that I did not really get any of it wrong, I just did my best with the knowledge and skills that I had available to me at the time, just as I believe we all do. No doubt I could have made better choices at times which may have saved me some pain, but pain is a part of healing too. Without darkness there can be no light. Also **just as the darkness and cold of winter helps us to appreciate the warmth and light of summer in this way the hard times make us appreciate the times when life is easy and overflows with beauty and joy.**[1] Gradually during this time of my life my perspective began to shift and as I allowed myself to heal I began to see the trauma of my youth not as an infected wound but as a beautiful wound that had gifted me with so much strength and empathy and compassion through the return journey to wholeness and health.

It seems when we are born into this world we are pure and whole but over time the experiences we have gradually mean we begin to believe we are not as we are meant to be. Our personalities develop based on reflections of who we are through other people in our lives and this seems to lead us away from the essence of who we really are. Paradoxically **our return to wholeness seems to be the unlearning of many lessons we were taught by other people and a return to a more childlike, innocent state of being.**[2] Perhaps this is what Jesus meant when he talked about children entering the kingdom of heaven?

Wounded

My time working at the college was drawing to a close, but before I left I was to be gifted with another challenge that would play a significant part in me discovering my life's work. It began when my head of department arrived in the office one day and placed a large ring binder folder on my desk. He explained it was the curriculum of a new qualification that the City and Guilds Examination Board were piloting for support workers in the homeless sector. As I had experience of working in the homeless sector he wanted me to deliver it. The thought of teaching adults meant that initially I was mortified and felt I would never be able to achieve this. It was a huge challenge for me and one which I reluctantly accepted and I began the daunting process of preparing the course step by step. It was a long and drawn out process as I struggled to understand the strange language the qualification was written in but, with time, it began to take shape and inevitably the day arrived when I found myself in front of twelve adults who were all looking at me and waiting for me to teach and guide them on their journey of learning. I felt totally out of my depth and I probably owe that group of students an apology for the quality of the course delivery. I made many mistakes but learnt quickly, largely to avoid the embarrassment of making them again!

One thing that really took the pressure off me was when I realised I did not have to know all the answers. It was okay for me to not know something and if a student asked me a question to which I did not know the answer, I would always make sure I found out and got back to them with the information. I discovered when I did not know something, for example, how to spell a word I was writing on the whiteboard I would ask the students and this seemed to put them at ease. By showing my own weaknesses and that I did not know everything my students would then feel it was ok to make mistakes and not know everything too. Over time I have found **it is invaluable to be open about our own learning journeys and share the things we are not good at with those that we are seeking to help.**[3]

By the time I had delivered the course for the fourth time I was in my stride and began to receive exceptional feedback from the mature students. I travelled around the country delivering the course in different locations and now see how this was a key step in building my self confidence and skills to be successful at designing and delivering my own training later. My self-belief grew with each course and gradually I felt less uncomfortable as a man that other adults looked to for support and guidance.   My focus was always on supporting the individual and in this way I saw the self-esteem of many of my students grow. I began to see very clearly that **a crucial part of raising self-esteem in others is supporting them to achieve things that they have previously thought unachievable.**[4] We are all capable of so much more than we often give ourselves credit for and sometimes someone else is much better placed to see our potential and the best route to take.

My own personal growth and learning continued too as I completed a drama-therapy qualification and was attending workshops on subjects such as the wisdom of the Native American and Maori elders. One talk by a man from New Zealand was very moving and there was one thing in particular he talked about that I will never forget.   He said: '**The greatest journey that a human being can ever make is the short distance from the head to the heart.**'[5] These words resonated deeply within me and I was intrigued by them. It took a long time before I really understood his words but gradually through personal experience I began to see the wisdom and relevance of them. We spend so much time in the world of thoughts and thinking and forget that our bodies and hearts have their own intelligence that we can tune into with practice. Sometimes we just feel in our hearts that something is true or needs to be done even though there is no rational logic or awareness that seems to support this sense of knowing. This journey of mine continues to this day as I live more and more from my heart.

As well as attending workshops and listening to inspirational speakers I was reading widely around spirituality, the teachings of Buddha, Jesus, the Hindu texts and many other areas. I was hungry for knowledge as well as experience of this whole new landscape of spirituality that was feeding and nourishing me. With a more direct focus on my work I also began to attend courses on coaching. It was while attending a coaching course that the mist again began to clear and my next stepping stone began to reveal itself.

I had enrolled on a life coaching course and was in attendance at the initial residential weekend. The first day was good and I began to see that many of the skills involved in coaching were ones I had developed through trial and error over the years of facilitating learning in my place of work at the college. This was a pleasant surprise and only confirmed to me I was on the right track with my understanding of how to create the ideal conditions for learning, growth and change. It was the second day of the residential however that became more significant.

The day began by introducing the agenda and to my initial dismay it focused on how to begin a career as an independent life coach. I had enrolled on the training to develop coaching skills in relation to my work at the college and initially cursed myself for not having read the course outline properly. But as the day progressed I began to ask myself the question: Why could I not work independently as a life coach? This possibility seemed to be asking for me to take a huge step in my self-belief but nevertheless the seed had been planted and, as is the way with seeds, in the darkness of my subconscious it began to germinate.

As I became increasingly disillusioned with my work at the college the realisation emerged that perhaps the time was coming when I could move on and perhaps that moving on involved me working for myself. If other people could do it then why couldn't I? I already had plenty of evidence to suggest when I set my mind to a goal I had the qualities necessary to achieve that goal. All I needed was the commitment to the goal and then, as has often been the case, when I focused my commitment the opportunities arose to help me achieve what it was that I wanted to achieve. The opportunity would indeed soon arise for me to take a leap of faith and I would find myself on my next stepping stone secure in the knowledge, as always, I was exactly where I was meant to be.

~

At home the flow of my relationship with Sally had seemed to slow right down to the point it was beginning to feel increasingly stagnant. This was not helped at all by the fact I found myself increasingly attracted to other women. We found ourselves locked in a cycle that was eroding our marriage. The more I allowed myself to be distracted by feelings for other women the more Sally shut down and closed herself to me. The more she closed herself to me the more I sought solace in the fantasy of how a relationship with another woman might heal the longing for connection and intimacy that I yearned for within me.

We were both reading books on how to heal relationships, seeking guidance from friends and we tried some couples counselling briefly too, but none of it really seemed to make much difference. Things went from bad to worse when Sally's father died.

For somebody who prides themselves on their ability to listen and empathise I think I did a pretty poor job. It was obviously a very distressing and difficult time for Sally and I was too wrapped up in dealing with my increasing lack of fulfilment at work and enjoying the distractions of my flirtatiousness. She was pretty much alone in her grief and I made the classic mistake of expecting her to pull herself together and get over it long before her grief had run its natural course. I still feel a sense of shame for this and hope that one day she can forgive me. The distance between us grew and we were increasingly becoming strangers living in the same house.

At work one day an email dropped into my inbox that was to make a huge difference and I hoped that it would make a difference to my relationship too. I am aware that when things are not nourishing me at work it has a direct impact on how I am at home, the two are interconnected and there is a strong connection in how fulfilled I feel in my work and who I am as a father and husband. I secretly hoped that my new career development might solve my problems at home too.

~

The email asked me to put forward a tender to design and deliver a coaching course directly aimed at working with disaffected young adults. I submitted the tender, attended a meeting in London and was soon informed I had been successful. This meant I could start working part-time at the college and was another crucial step in building my confidence for the transition into self employment.

Again, I found my new task very challenging as it was unlike anything I had done before, but step by step I put the course together and began delivering it to managers in the homeless sector. The direct result of this new venture was I began to see by comparison how unsatisfactory my work at the college had become and, increasingly, the three days I spent there each week became tedious to the extent that time dragged. This was a sure sign it was time to get out and I hoped my new found aspirations to work for myself might be enough to save my marriage. Sally had recently acquired an inheritance from the death of her father and the idea was I would hand in my notice at the college and her father's money would help us get by while I built my own business. Things were not helped at home by the fact I became emotionally involved with a colleague at the college. To be honest, my infatuations with women was becoming a habit I felt I had no control over. I began to sense the end for Sally and me was near and this was confirmed by a discussion with my father one day while he was visiting.

His marriage had come to an end when, at the age of 68, he had decided to leave my stepmother. They had not been happy together for a long time and were now living separately and going through a divorce. I did not want to grow old with a woman out of fear of being alone and I knew Sally and I were not destined to grow old together. My father's decision to leave my stepmother at his age had an impact on me and I confided in him things were not good between Sally and me. He shared with me he would not judge me and that he would still love me as his son whatever I chose to do but I should think carefully on the implications before I made any decisions. I am aware his response meant that somehow I had his blessing and, although this was by no means essential, it meant the increasingly common thought of not being with Sally began to feel like it might become a reality.

One day Sally and I were sitting in our back garden. Our lack of connection had again come to a head and we were discussing the increasing distance between us. Often in similar discussions Sally would lament how she did not feel she could continue living in the same way and that living with a man who didn't really love her fully was destroying her. My usual response would be to remind her of how far we had come and that I would try to do better and we would overcome this challenge as we had overcome many challenges together, but this time I did not say this. When she said she couldn't continue in the same way I just said 'ok, I will go.'

I hadn't planned to say these words as I hadn't felt I had really made up my mind this was the only course of action, but the words came out of my mouth. To my surprise Sally offered no resistance and that was that. Little did I know the impact those four simple little words 'ok, I will go' would have on my life.

For some strange reason I had this romantic notion we would have some kind of Hollywood separation where we would look back over the years at all the adventures and wonderful times we had shared. We would forgive each other for our shortcomings and just put it down to learning. We would perhaps make love one last time and then go our separate ways. As it happened it wasn't quite like that. From that pivotal moment in the garden Sally shut me out emotionally. I don't blame her and though I didn't really understand at the time why it had to be that way. I fully understand now that she was doing what she had to in order to survive the great emotional upheaval that was to follow.

It was almost the beginning of the school summer holidays and she asked if I would stay until the kids went back to school. It was agreed the boys would stay with her which made sense as I would still have to make a living and I was going to be busy with my new self-employed career. I was happy to stay until the end of the summer and this would give me time to sort out some accommodation, a new car and practicalities. The issue of money inevitably came up and I offered to pay, what seemed to me to be a generous amount of maintenance for the boys. I was adamant from the beginning the separation would have as little impact on my sons as possible. It was clear to me I was leaving Sally and not my boys. After a brief discussion it was agreed that Sally would keep her father's inheritance and I would have a small sum of savings we had in the bank. I was aware that while I had been building my career and skills Sally had been at home bringing up our boys. She was a wonderful mother and I know those years of care and love from Sally have had a massive positive impact on how secure and content both Ash and Sol now are. The inheritance was hers and was some payment for all those years of unpaid work she did as a mother. I have always known in some ways the job she did at home was as important, if not more, than the work I was doing and getting paid for. I was not concerned about money and I thought work would come rolling in but it turned out the transition to self-employment was not as straight forward as I had initially thought.

Now that Sally and I were no longer officially together as partners I wasted no time in putting my new found freedom to good use and pretty soon was exploring the world of online dating. It was a satisfactory distraction from the collapse of my marriage and at last it felt as if I was free to make legitimate connections with other women. I was quite excited by the beginning of my new life and was insensitive to how Sally was feeling. For some reason she began to grieve the death of our marriage straight away while the reality of it had not yet hit me. I distracted myself with preparations for my new life, my career plans and virtual relationships on the internet. The reality of the situation only hit me in the last two weeks of our time together. They were two of the worst weeks of my life.

We had booked a holiday in Corfu many months earlier and not wanting to waste the money we decided that we would all still go. Oh God, how I wished I had stayed at home as on holiday there were no distractions, there was no escape from what was happening and the gravity of the massive upheaval that my life was about to undergo quickly sank in.

Sally understandably wouldn't let me near her and insisted we slept in separate rooms after I had made it clear I still wanted to be intimate with her. Despite the fact I had been the one to say I would go all-encompassing feelings of rejection, abandonment and fear arose in me. It was too hot to walk in Corfu and endless hours were spent around the pool torturing myself with destructive thoughts as I was too distraught to even focus on a book.

One morning I had gone for an early walk before the full heat of the day had begun and I was walking on the beach looking for pretty pebbles. My focus shifted to looking for heart shaped stones and I scoured the beach for some time. I was just about to leave and I had found nothing that resembled a heart when I happened to glance up at the clay cliff. There, carefully pushed into the sticky clay was a perfect heart shaped stone about the size of my hand. I stood and stared at it in disbelief for a while and saw it had been broken down the middle and had been pushed back together. I crumbled to the sand and sobbed, it was as if for the first time I was seeing and feeling the full extent of the pain of my poor heart. I felt wretched and scared and alone and when I thought about the impending end of life with my family I couldn't help but wonder what I had done.

Every day in Corfu seemed to last forever and I counted the days down looking forward to the end of the prison that the hotel and pool had become. Although, at a glance, it appeared I was in paradise my state of mind meant that I was in my own personal hell. I was once again reminded by this painful experience that **our inner world, our emotional state and state of mind are the factors which determine our happiness and that things and places really have little bearing on the quality of our lives.**[6] Eventually the holiday from hell came to an end. The boys knew that things were far from right between us and we had already told them that I was leaving but I suspect it wasn't the best holiday they have ever had either and they did not seem to be disappointed to be going home.

On the plane back I was hit with an almighty blow to my heart as Sol talked with excitement about how he was looking forward to getting back to his bedroom and all his toys and I realised I was going back to pack my suitcase and leave my home and family. Once again I felt as if I was alone and destitute. The pain was almost unbearable and was eased only by the numbness that seemed to be spreading through my chest.

On arriving back in England the plan was I would stay the night as it was late and we had been travelling since early that morning. I would move into the new shared house I had arranged to rent the next day. As the car pulled up outside to what was no longer my home I knew I had to go straight away. I was aware some friends were at a festival in Dorset at the time and I hurriedly threw some things in my new little

Peugeot and drove into the night. I am quite surprised now I arrived at my destination safely as I struggled to see through the tears that filled my eyes and ran down my face. I cried nearly the whole way there and drove recklessly fast with the windows wound down and music blaring out of the stereo. At the festival I was a mess. I cried and cried in just about every workshop I attended and found a little solace from the few beautiful friends I knew and some strangers who accepted me as I was and allowed me to feel my grief without any judgment.

The festival soon came to an end and it was time for me to return and pack my things properly and get out of my home. I spoke with Sally and she made sure she and the boys were not in while I gathered my belongings. It is hard to describe the feelings in my body as I hurriedly loaded up my car, but I think it was the pinnacle of my suffering as the reality of what was happening tore through me in waves of nausea and grief resulting in a sick feeling in my stomach. I closed the door behind me and drove away from my home where the woman who I had shared 14 years of my life lived, with my two beautiful sons.

In the fog of emotion nothing is ever clear[7] but over time I have come to understand what actually happened to my marriage and why it was that, in effect, I sabotaged it. It came as no surprise to me it was all connected to the early loss of my mother and it is a well known fact our relationship with our parents will have a large impact on our subsequent relationships. I believe that by the time I had lost my mother and Aunty Carol and much of the love from my stepmother I had built a protective wall around my heart. The purpose of this wall was to protect me by preventing me from fully loving because my experience was that whoever I loved and became dependent on seemed to leave me and if this were to happen again I would be left with more suffering and pain. While I was with Sally I was doing my best to dismantle this wall to allow me to feel her love for me and in turn allow me to fully love her. I think I experienced love up to a point but when things got challenging and there was the opportunity to dismantle the bulk of the wall by daring to surrender to love fully I got fearful and my mind started telling me all sorts of reasons why I should leave Sally rather than take the risk. My courage to dismantle the wall was eventually eclipsed by my fear and eventually I succumbed to my mind's thoughts along the lines of 'the grass is greener on the other side' or 'she is not the right one' or 'you best leave her before she becomes more dependent on you and you hurt her even more because you are bound to leave at some point.' I believe she was not the right person and the time was not right for me to allow love in and I was only really beginning to understand that **to feel the love of another we need to truly love and accept ourselves.**[8]

Unfortunately, this insight and the courage to transcend my fear came too late to save my marriage and of course Sally's issues and wounds around relationships with men all added to the emotional confusion at the time. Since my marriage I have had the privilege to be in relationship with a couple of very beautiful women and I have also caused them and myself pain again because of this old wound. It is only now I find myself fully able to delete this software that was installed in my mind and body so many years ago. I understand that my mind had my best interests at heart and was trying to protect me from further pain but I refuse to live my life in this way anymore. Again, the power of commitment has come to my aid and before long I was able to heal this wound once and for all, but I am not yet at that place in the story - there is more to tell of the time of my separation from Sally. It is hard for me to comprehend as I sit here but it seems I still needed more lessons of pain and suffering before I was ready to learn the lesson of letting go of my fear and opening to love.

My new home was not a home. It was smelly, damp and cold but it was all I could afford. The best thing about it was it was on top of the Malvern Hills and my room had a window that faced east and I was able to see the most beautiful sunrises most mornings. I would focus my intent with the rising of the sun on the new beginning and the end of my grief I knew would come eventually. As well as the spectacular view my new abode was only a mile up the road from Sally's place which meant I could easily see my boys and they would not feel I was far away.

People often talk about the terrible damage that divorce does to children but from the outset I was determined to find a different way. It was crystal clear to me that divorcing Sally was not an excuse to give up my commitment to my sons and I was sure that **divorce does not have to mean huge emotional wounds inflicted on children.**[9]

It is now nearly three years since I left Sally and I believe I have achieved my goal of minimising the impact of our separation on my sons. Behaviour is usually a key indicator that things are not well with a young person as they struggle to articulate what is happening for them and so communicate through their actions and attitude. To date there has not been any significant change in the behaviour of Sol or Ash. I think this is due to a few key factors. Firstly, that Sally and I never abused each other verbally or physically. There were times when there was a bad atmosphere in the house but there was no great build up or atmosphere of anger or hatred. We kept our discussions and pain between ourselves as much as we could. We made sure we explained to the boys what was happening and I would still be totally there for them even though I was moving out and that I wanted to see them as much as possible. Also, I have never used the boys as a way of getting at Sally. On the contrary, I have always told them that Sally is a good mum and to be good for her and treat her with the respect she deserves. I like to think that Sally has acted in a similar way and the evidence would suggest this is true. Perhaps lastly, and most importantly, although I know there are ways in which I could have been a better Dad, I now make a point of telling them often that I love them and that I am proud of them. This is the truth and I am blessed to have a good relationship with both of my boys which I hope will last until the end of my days.

Lessons for Life

1. Just as the darkness and cold of winter helps us to appreciate the warmth and light of summer in the same way, the hard times make us appreciate the times when life is easy and overflows with beauty and joy.

2. Our return to wholeness seems to be the unlearning of many lessons that we were taught by other people and a return to a more childlike state of being.

3. It is invaluable to be open about our own learning journeys and the things we are not good at with those we are seeking to help.

4. A crucial part of raising self-esteem in others is supporting them to achieve things that they have previously thought unachievable.

5. The greatest journey that a human being can ever make is the short distance from the head to the heart.

6. Our inner world, our emotional state and state of mind are the factors which determine our happiness and that things and places really have little bearing on the quality of our lives.

7. In the fog of emotion nothing is ever clear.

8. To feel the love of another we need to truly love and accept ourselves.

9. Divorce does not have to mean huge emotional wounds inflicted on children.

Chapter Seven – Lessons of the Heart

I suppose it took about two years before I stopped feeling like damaged goods. I felt as if I had 'Broken Man' tattooed on my forehead and that it was plain for everybody to see how I was vulnerable and tender. The situation was not helped by the fact that making a living as a coach and trainer was not as straight forward as I had thought it would be.

I joined a business networking group and every Wednesday I would force myself out of bed at 5.45 am and put on my smart clothes to attend the breakfast meetings. I felt very out of place at first in this environment as I had no business experience or network to engage with. I did my best to find other people business referrals and contributed in the ways I could. Most Wednesdays I would return home, put my jeans on and go walking on the hills. I had no work and had very little motivation and I found great solace on the hills. Somehow they seemed to ease the dull ache of loneliness and failure that gnawed from within.

In time I had my website designed and began to be more proactive as I gradually learnt about how the world of business worked. If I could rewind time I might have gone about things differently. I would have read extensively and researched much more; I would have learnt about marketing, sales, social networking, media, public speaking and book keeping instead of spending so much time in my bedroom writing training courses and workshops. For some reason in my naivety I overlooked this preparation and so the steep learning curve began. I made some classic mistakes along the way and paid the price of struggling to find enough work while my small sum of savings rapidly began to disappear. One of the best mistakes I made was a mail shot marketing campaign. I had some lovely glossy (and expensive) fliers designed and printed and posted them out to all the secondary schools in Hereford and Worcester. I expected to just be able to sit by the telephone while the bookings came in. What a fool I was. If I had done everything else right I would have been lucky to secure any sales without making follow up calls but I had also made a more significant error.

A few days after I posted the information I received a call from a school who kindly informed me I had not put enough postage on the envelope I had sent them. They had had to go to the Post Office and pay the difference to get the mail. I was devastated to find out there was such a thing as a large letter postage stamp and I had only affixed ordinary first class stamps! In order to remedy the situation as best as I could I sent letters of apology out to all the schools with stamps to cover the short fall in cost but the damage had already been done. Who was going to hire a trainer that could not even handle the simple task of posting a letter? Another lesson learnt, the hard way too I might add!

People say that bad luck (or challenges) comes in threes. It would seem that sometimes they are right. I was already coping with the loss of my family and a lonely existence as well as discovering that making a living was not going to be the walk in the park that I had expected, when my third challenge presented itself to me.

As a single man I was quite active in online dating although, for the most part, I was discovering most of the women seemed to be terrified of a real date and that virtual dating was the name of the game. I met some very strange women online and few of them developed into real dates. One date that did materialise ended up being very sleazy as we met in London, had dinner and then went back to my hotel and had sex. It was most unsatisfactory and the morning after I excused myself from more sex explaining I had to do my Tai Chi practice. My friend had given me some Viagra in an attempt to help me get the best of the situation but I only took a little of it and it had little effect on my performance. I might have taken more but I was being filmed for a coaching video the next day and I was concerned it would not look good if I had a suspiciously large bulge in my trousers for the filming!

Being a responsible sort of chap I decided the right thing to do was to have a test at the sexual health clinic after my experience in London as I had not used any protection. I think I probably quite liked the fact a visit to the clinic was a sort of statement I was able to have sex with whoever I wanted and that I had. The nurse at the clinic asked permission to test for other diseases that were not sexually transmitted, to which I responded that while they were at it they could test me for whatever they wanted to. On leaving the clinic I was told that if everything was clear I would get a text message. If there were any problems or complications I would get a phone call asking me to come in for an appointment.

It was Christmas Eve and I had met a lovely woman who was happy to be with me even though I was still very much 'damaged goods.' It was a short relationship but I am very grateful for the love and care she showed me in those dark days. I was sat up on her bed when a message came through on my mobile phone. It was a voicemail so I rang and listened to the message. It took a few moments for the words to sink in. It was from the nurse at the sexual health clinic. I was to get in touch as soon as possible to arrange a time to come in for a consultation. It felt like a bad dream but as the reality sank in, wide awake fear gripped me and tears of desperation began to flow. Why me? What disease did I have? Other similar questions raced through my mind. Merry Christmas

Miguel! Just when I thought life could not get any more challenging the news from my mobile phone seemed so cruel and unfair.

When I attended my appointment at the clinic I was told that I had Hepatitis C. At least it was not AIDS and the doctor reassured me that there was an 80% success rate of fully curing it if I were to take a six month course of drugs. It was all such a surprise because although emotionally and psychologically I still felt broken I was not aware of any physical symptoms that would suggest my liver was not well. The results of the test were conclusive and I left the clinic to go away and do some research as to whether I could heal myself with complimentary therapies and alternative medicine. There was some evidence to suggest this was possible but I would have to totally change my lifestyle if this were to succeed. After a few months of half-heartedly trying the alternative approach my blood test still showed that, although there was some improvement, my liver was still riddled with the Hepatitis C virus. I was reminded by the doctors if the issue were not addressed then it would result in sclerosis of the liver which would, in turn, lead to liver failure with a liver transplant being the only remedy. This was not a very pleasant proposition.

Hepatitis C is passed on through contaminated blood and in trying to discover where I had caught it the doctors asked if I practiced anal sex or used needles to take drugs. As the answer to both these rather embarrassing questions was no, it would appear the most likely place I picked it up was from a dirty tattoo needle. I had two tattoos; one I had twenty years earlier and the other ten years earlier. It appeared I had been walking around with Hepatitis C for the last ten or twenty years while it steadily and secretly multiplied in my liver. I realised that it was probably responsible for the low energy I felt much of the time and even though I felt physically okay the thought of liver failure led me to decide it was time to embark on the six month course of drugs.

I had a load of Ribavirin tablets to take each day and had to give myself an injection in the belly once a week of Interferon. I went to the hospital once a month to have tests which confirmed the steady decrease of the virus in my blood. The specialist nurses were lovely. I felt in safe hands and I became rather fond of them. The list of side effects from the drugs was long and although I glanced at them I decided I did not want to focus on the possibility of complications and that ignorance might be best. To begin with I didn't notice any side effects but about three months into the course of treatment things changed.

The first thing that I noticed was that I became short of breath and was wheezy. Then I began to feel itchy and within a week I was covered in a red rash that became incredibly uncomfortable. It began on my back but quickly spread to the whole of my body. The soreness meant that sleep became almost impossible as the warmth of the duvet only made matters worse and I would lay awake at night feeling incredibly itchy, alone, exhausted and desperate. My self-esteem plummeted and I became depressed.

The doctors and nurses had never seen anything like it at the hospital and although they were kind and prescribed some creams it made little difference. It was a tough time and while I felt as if I just wanted to stay at home and hide from the world I was forced to continue to work at building my business. I struggled on and was supported by great love from my family and close friends. Without them I know the whole experience would have been much worse and once again I found myself full of gratitude and I feel their love was helping to dismantle the wall around my heart.

I think the lowest point came for me one evening in early December almost a year after the initial diagnosis. I had decided earlier in the year before I got ill, that I wanted to experience a different culture, see a bit of the world and do something that would help those less fortunate than myself. I had been fundraising for 6 months to go to Nicaragua with a charity organization who served the poor. I had not expected to get so ill from the Hepatitis C treatment and, although I did eventually go, I had to postpone the trip for 6 months while my health improved and my body rebalanced itself. In December I had arranged a fundraising event at my friend's wine bar with food, music and some stalls. On that particular evening I felt wretched. I knew that I would have to take centre stage and play host. It was not that I did not appreciate the support of so many lovely people but being in the spotlight was the last place that I wanted to be. My skin was incredibly uncomfortable by this time, I felt ugly, exhausted and miserable.

I guess that **it is at times when we are on our knees, close to desperation and we find the strength to carry on that define who we are.**[1] I thought about phoning my friend at the wine bar to explain I would not be able to come due to illness but I could not let all those people down. I put on my best shirt and drove the short distance to the Wine Bar. The evening was very successful and we raised the last sum of money needed to make my trip to Nicaragua possible. I did my bit with the microphone and circulated amongst all the lovely people who had bothered to turn out to support me in my venture. I guess there were feelings of uncertainty at this time too about whether I would ever be well enough to undertake the trip and I felt that in some way I was asking for sponsorship under false pretences. With hindsight I should have just told everybody about my health issues but, for some reason, I felt ashamed and did not have the courage to share what was going on for me. At last the evening came to an end and I returned to the security and isolation of my home and another sleepless night.

In January 2010 I gave myself the last injection of liquid that was making me feel so ill and also ridding me of the virus. By the time I received the test results from the hospital to say that I no longer had Hepatitis C I was feeling very low. Months with very little sleep had taken their toll and I was grateful that I had not managed to win any training contracts as I would have been too ill to fulfil them. By now my savings had all gone and I was forced to swallow my pride and borrow money from my family. I had never been in debt before but it was made easier by the fact they obviously wanted to help and it was a way of showing their love.

Strangely, at my lowest point another beautiful woman came into my life whose name was Linda. It was incredible to me that she found me attractive as I felt so hideous. She did not see the ugliness of my skin as I did and instead seemed to see beyond this. In my vulnerability I was so grateful for the kindness and love that she showed me. I felt as if I had so little to give but for some reason she wanted me. She was a beautiful light in the gloom that my life had become and I will always have a place in my heart for her.

We spent over a year together and gradually with the passing of time, her love and patience, I healed in many ways. When we first met my skin was such that we could not make love and I was understandably distressed at how slowly things got better. When faced with toxic overload the body's natural course of action is to expel the toxins as much as possible through the liver and kidneys but my body had not been able to cope with the amount of strong medication with an impaired liver and so it was forced to store the toxins in places away from primary organs. Over the years my body gradually released these toxins it had stored. My recovery seemed painfully slow. After a little while my skin became less sore and my sleep gradually improved and with this came the lifting of the dark cloud of depression.

As my health gradually returned so did my confidence and self-esteem in the light of my relationship with Linda. She too had experienced great challenges as a child and for the first time in her life she began to share the ordeals that she had suffered. I was honoured she felt safe enough to share her pain for the first time with me and together the two of us supported each other's journey from damaged and broken goods to more whole and healthy human beings. It never ceases to amaze me that so many people have heart wrenching stories to tell and yet so often we never hear their stories as our society does not encourage us to speak openly of our wounds, but rather we should conceal them as if they were something to be ashamed of. When we share our wounds it is a gift to the people we tell and it helps heal our wounds at the same time. In my time with Linda there was more learning for me and pain once again played its part as I continued to learn the lessons of love and fear. This time the pain was a direct result of my own making and was invaluable in helping me see more clearly the path to my healing. I made a choice that led to pain and in the pain that it caused I saw once and for all how not to be.

This lesson began with a flattering email from a woman thanking me for an inspirational seminar I had given at a small conference.   The email quickly turned into flirtatious exchanges and pretty soon my ego was so flattered I became intent on meeting her. I shared this with Linda who I was still having a relationship with at the time. I pretty much told her I was going to meet this woman and that it was possible the meeting may involve physical intimacy. She seemed to be ok with this on the condition that it was ok for her to invite a male friend of hers to stay and this may also involve physical intimacy. I agreed and the wheels were set in motion. We were exploring an open relationship. It seemed to me at the time perhaps I could not fully give myself to one woman because that was not my path or that was not how it was meant to be. Open relationships had been something I was curious about and I guess it was something I needed to explore or get out of my system.

However, it did not go quite as I planned! I drove down to Devon and met up with my email companion. As soon as we were together there was a sinking feeling in my stomach as I realised that I felt no physical attraction for her and to make matters worse it was clear she felt differently. I should have left straight away but for some reason I stayed and before long we were in bed together. I tried my best to 'perform' for her but all the time I was thinking about Linda with her friend. It felt a bit as if I was allowing myself to be raped and I felt terrible. Eventually as the afternoon wore on I mustered the courage to tell her the truth about how I was feeling. She was very upset and I saw how my own selfishness and foolishness had directly caused her a great deal of pain. On the drive home I felt terribly ashamed and found some solace in the fact I would soon be back with Linda. I would tell her how sorry I was and that I had learnt my lesson and soon everything would be back to normal.

To my utter dismay on calling Linda she told me I could not come round. She had had such a great night with her friend they were going to spend another night together. I was devastated. Linda really had given me a great big dose of my own medicine which I found very hard to swallow. I spent the night alone torturing myself with images of her with another man. In the darkness I saw, for the first time, the pain that I had caused Sally and in the silence I asked for forgiveness. Although I take full responsibility for what happened with Linda, for some reason I still felt an incredibly strong sense of betrayal. When Linda and I later talked about what had happened I saw I had hurt her so much by even considering being with another woman she acted from a place of anger and wanted to hurt me back. She did a really good job of it and I am glad now she was so thorough as I will never go down that path again.

As my immediate health issues resolved themselves and Linda and I did our best to put the incident behind us, my deeper, and as yet unhealed, emotional wounds began to increasingly manifest in our relationship. The essence of this was I was still scared to open my heart to the love of this woman too and I found the nagging and somewhat familiar voice in my head became louder and louder telling me she was not right for me and I should leave her as I was not able to give her the commitment she needed. I left her a few times but I did have deep feelings for her and her love for me was so great that she always persuaded me to come back.

I was still obsessed with the thought there was a woman somewhere who I would meet and I would know in my heart it was with her I would take the ultimate risk and give all of myself to, including my heart. I also knew there was work I would have to do alone, without the support of a woman, which would empower me. I knew I would have to learn to stand in my own power as a man, independently and at peace with myself; I needed to learn to love myself fully before I could enter a healthy relationship with another that would not involve co-dependency. Gradually this commitment began to grow within me. The time was coming to let go of my fear and take the risk and to love fully but I was not quite ready, the time was not quite right, though I began to sense that it was not far away.

~

About six months after I had left Sally and the boys I had moved back in to the family home we previously shared. Sally had bought a property nearby with her inheritance and moved in with the boys. I moved back in to the rented accommodation which was much better than the shared house where I had lived when we had first separated. At first it was very difficult as I was surrounded by memories of the life that I had once had there, but being faced with the ghosts of the past on a daily basis meant I had to deal with it and over time memories of the past stopped stimulating painful feelings. My understanding is **emotions serve a purpose and when we have the courage to feel what we need to feel this brings a sense of freedom**[2] as eventually the painful feelings cease to arise once they have been fully expressed.

I painted and decorated and made the house into my home. I had not expected to be able to return and it was a welcome surprise. One of the best things about it was that it was a short walk from where Sally and my sons were living so it was easy for Ash and Sol to come over any time or when it was their time to be with me. They would stay on alternate weekends and little Sol would spend the night with me on Wednesdays. I loved having them about. Ash was 15 and very independent by this time and Sol was a lovely bright little being full of life and mischief. When they were with me my house felt so much more like a home than when I was alone. It was hard at first when they went back to Sally's after a weekend with me but gradually I became more accustomed to this. I allowed myself to let go of any feelings of guilt. I was paying my maintenance money from borrowed money and doing my best to be a loving father. Ash and I were on good terms, we developed a good text relationship and I would ring Sol regularly and see him quite often as his best friend lived next door to me. My beautiful boys, of whom I am so proud, seemed to have come through pretty much unscathed from the divorce of their parents. I know **our children have their own journey and their own lessons to learn**[3] and everything they experience will shape the men they will become just as my experiences have shaped me. I hope the divorce does not cause them too many issues in the future. Maybe someday they will tell me about their experience of me leaving and only time will tell the full extent of how it affected them.

~

Having postponed the trip once already I made preparations for Central America. My time in Nicaragua was something that I needed to do and, as with all my experiences, I have no regrets. Linda and I were only just getting over our painful encounter with open relationships when I left and I missed her terribly while I was away. I left her sleeping like an angel in my bed in the middle of the night and embarked on my three week adventure.

My fellow volunteers were kind people intent on making a difference to those less fortunate and this desire to serve was something which was also growing within me. However, their outlook on life was very different to mine and I found myself unable to connect with them on a deep level. I enjoyed the church services and the celebration of life but their understanding of God was very different to mine. I think that much of Jesus' teachings have been misunderstood and that dogma and religion are responsible for so much war and hatred and suffering.   I believe we are all entitled to our beliefs and it was clear that my fellow volunteers' beliefs were different to mine.

The work in the tropical heat was hard and my health was still not back to one hundred per cent. Some of the time was spent building a concrete path for a community that lived around the rubbish tip, from which most of the people supplemented their incredibly poor and basic existence. The other focus was on working with the children in their small schools and running holiday clubs when the schools were not open. I was acutely aware though that although the Nicaraguans were financially very poor they had a richness in spirit that was beautiful to witness. The majority of the people we worked with lived in small wooden shacks with pigs and dogs wandering freely around and at first sight it seemed a miserable existence. But because, for the most part, they knew no different they seemed quite content and there were lots of smiles especially from the many beautiful, barefoot children. I saw suffering too and witnessed violence between different ethnic gangs in the town. There was a murder while we were there and we were not allowed out after dark because it was not safe. One night somebody broke into where we slept and stole some money. The armed guard had unfortunately fallen asleep that night and at times it was a scary place to be but it was nowhere near as scary as some things I have experienced in my New Age Traveller days!

The many hours I spent with the children are my fondest memories. We danced and sang with them and they coloured in pictures and made masks. These simple activities were a great treat for them.   Their aliveness and smiling faces nourished my spirit while my body struggled under the oppressive heat with a skin infection and stomach bug which I developed. My fondest Nicaraguan memory was of a little girl called Anna Maria. During a break at the holiday club she was eating a mango and I commented to her in Spanish on the beautiful smell of the sun ripened fruit. She beamed at me with her dark brown eyes and shiny white teeth. A few moments later she found me again with some other children and offered me a mango from her packed lunch. I was so touched by her generosity and kindness and knowing that although she had so little to give she was willing to share the little food she had with me. Her act touched me deeply and reminded me of the potential kindness within all human beings. It is often **when we have little to share, what we do share becomes something enormously touching and valuable.**[4] I will always be grateful to Anna Maria for reminding me of this truth.

They say when you die that all the significant moments of your life flash before you. I know that if this is true Anna Maria's beautiful face with her arm outstretched, mango in hand will be one of those pictures. I wonder what she is doing now. I hope life is gentle with her and that her life will not be too hard, although I suspect that my wishes may be in vain.

As I made the long flight back to England I pondered on my Nicaraguan experience and one thing became clear for me. Whatever my life's work was it was not in Nicaragua. I now had a sense that my destiny lay nearer to my home and when the mist was ready to clear and reveal my next stepping stone it would be related to the work I was already doing in my native country. I was glad of this insight as it meant I could be close to my sons as I had been prepared to live elsewhere, away from my children, if I knew for sure that is where I was meant to be. I was somewhat relieved that I could fulfil my commitment and be near my sons until they grew up and no longer needed me to be such an immediate part of their lives.

On my return from Nicaragua I rested. My body healed and my reunion with Linda was sweet. We still had ups and downs largely related to my fear of commitment, but for the first time since my separation, I began to let go of the belief that I was damaged goods. On the contrary, I was a survivor and I was coming through another incredibly challenging time of my life. I had learnt so much about compassion and empathy and pain.

~

I like to think of what I learnt in this part of my life as lessons of the heart; perhaps the most important lessons we can ever have. Through the richness of life's experiences I was discovering what I did not want in my life. I was discovering what was important to me and through a process of elimination I felt I was coming closer to an understanding of my life. I began to see more clearly how everything that made up my life was leading me somewhere. Life was not just some random meaningless exercise loosely related to procreation. It was not yet clear but my life was about connection with myself in order to connect authentically with others. It was about finding the gift buried within the wounds from my past. It was about service to humanity through openness and honesty and integrity. Things were coming into focus and at times waves of gratitude and aliveness would permeate my being. There was more work to be done and I knew that the next steps would reveal themselves before long; all I had to do was be patient, continue my learning and keep the faith.

Lessons for Life

1. It is at times when we are on our knees, close to desperation and we find the strength to carry on that define who we are.

2. Emotions serve a purpose and when we have the courage to feel what we need to feel this brings a sense of freedom.

3. Our children have their own journey and their own lessons to learn.

4. When we have little to share, what we do share becomes something enormously touching and valuable.

Chapter Eight – New Beginnings

My business was ticking along. I had secured some reasonable sized training contracts and I managed to pay back some of the money I had borrowed from my family. I was doing some voluntary work in schools, working with children and training those that worked with particularly vulnerable young people. I also did some coaching with both young people and adults and was beginning to speak publicly a little. I loved working directly with clients in groups or individually but still found the sales and marketing part of being self-employed challenging. I began to do less networking as I saw I had little in common with so many business people who were focused primarily on making a living.

I was increasingly working with people who were ripe for change. This was the aspect of my work I was feeling most passionate about. Some were care leavers, others were ex-offenders and some were just your average kind of person who realised it was time to 'step up'. They were committed to being the best that they could be and were often altruists, keen to help others. They saw, like me, that in overcoming adversity they had become more of who they really were. These people were incredibly nourishing to work with and because of my life journey I saw I was ideally placed to help them overcome their demons and perhaps see their demons were in fact angels! There are few prizes bigger than enabling someone to see the gift in adversity and I know that as my vocation develops I will be working more and more with these brave, inspirational characters.

~

Although things at work became clearer and more in focus, the same was not true of my relationship with Linda. I increasingly began to question whether I was with her because I really wanted to be with her or because I really did not want to be alone. As I look back now I know it was a bit of both and although we had been good for each other up to a point I could not see her in my future. There were many ways in which we were well suited, but there were also ways in which she did not nourish me. It is important for a man to know that his woman believes in him and his ability to achieve his goals but I knew Linda felt I was aiming too high and did not seem to fully understand my work was not about doing a job or making money. It was something that was an integral part of my being and my reason for being alive. Although she was very beautiful and was a wonderful lover I did not have a sense Linda was the woman to walk with me through the next part of my life.

Since Sally and I had separated I had spent little time totally on my own without a girlfriend, although working and living alone meant I spent many days in my own company. Over time I began to be more comfortable with myself and I know there was great healing during this time of solitude. I questioned whether I needed to spend time without a woman by my side and found very soon after the end of a relationship I would find myself involved with another beautiful woman. I guess I was manifesting this.

I may have been deluding myself and it may been that I needed time without a woman in my life, but it seemed to me I had spent almost the first eighteen years of my life without the softness and loving care that is part of the beauty of the feminine. When I remember this it is not surprising I feel such a strong attraction to the feminine. I can survive on my own but it always feels that something big and beautiful is missing when I do not have a woman to share my life with. There are no rigid rules in this game of life and I accepted that fact the quality of my life was greatly enhanced by the presence of the feminine and I stopped giving myself a hard time about it. Although it was a relief to have finally come to terms with this there was still the sense I had a final obstacle to clear, a wound to heal that meant there was a part of me that was holding back and not fully opening up my heart to the full potential of love between two human beings. The opportunity to heal this wound and let go of a grief that had been buried deep within me was soon to come and, interestingly, it came about through the love and kindness of men and not women!

~

A few years previously I had made a commitment to having authentic men in my life. For as long as I could remember I had been frustrated by my inability to connect with other men. I had always found it easier to connect with women and found I had very little in common with most of the men I met. It is true I had received a great deal from my teachers Brendon, Peter and Juan but when my apprenticeship with them had run its course and I had learned what I needed, they had all but disappeared from my life.

My friend Mark was an exception to this. I met him many years earlier on a spiritual retreat and we stayed close friends. He was gentler than most men, in tune with his feminine and it was refreshing to be in his company as I could totally be myself with him. We shared our adventures as we navigated the inner landscapes of love and fear and relationships and what it was to be a man.

I had other male friends too. Roger was one of my oldest friends. We met when I was 19 and we spent many evenings together where we would invariably get horrendously drunk and stoned and talk about things which seemed very profound at the time, only to find the morning would bring a hangover and little recollection of the night before. For many years this was the best experience I had of relating to other men but this kind of friendship no longer nourishes me. Roger is a good man but he struggles with relationships and refuses to see it is his patterns and beliefs that ruin his relationships. He is not inclined to take responsibility and change himself and his anger and disrespect for women becomes an increasing obstacle to our friendship and means that over time we continue to grow apart.

People come and go in our lives and their presence always brings a gift or a lesson of some shape or form.[1] Through a series of chance encounters I was introduced to a man called Pete whose presence was to act like a catalyst. Pete is involved in setting up a charity whose focus is to organise Rites of Passage adventure weekends and mentoring for boys (Journeyman UK). There are no rites of passage within our culture and I had long been aware there was no real guidance for boys into the world of men, or what it actually means to be an authentic man in the world we live in today. This work felt very much in alignment with my own values and ideas and I began to watch from the sidelines as the organisation gathered men to volunteer and make the project happen. At first I did not have the motivation to travel the distance to attend the meetings, but eventually my curiosity got the better of me and I found myself volunteering to staff the first weekend that would initiate nine boys into the world of authentic masculinity.

It was the beginning of my experience of being with a tribe, a clan of men who were all prepared to give their time and energy with the aim of helping to create a generation of boys who would grow up to be authentic, honest and loving. A generation of boys that would know how to chart the inner landscape of demons and shadows that every man faces when he has the courage and awareness to look within. There was a sense of coming home when I found myself surrounded by these kind of men.

The boys' Rites of Passage Adventure Weekend was a powerful experience. I saw a great transformation in the self-esteem and spirit of the boys over such a short period of time but what was just as profound was the healing effect the weekend had on me. It brought me into balance I suppose. Where previously my focus had always been in search of myself through my relationships with women I found myself having an incredibly powerful and positive experience of masculine energy. In that space, somehow, I had a greater sense of who I was as a man. Everybody worked together, supported each other and yet each man was also individual and treated with respect.

Many of the men were involved in an organisation called The Mankind Project and my curiosity began to grow as to what this was all about. If these beautiful men that I felt so comfortable with were involved then perhaps it was something for me? My best friend Mark had already been on the Mankind Project residential weekend and he recommended that I go. I initially dismissed the idea, thinking I did not need the experience, and that my personal growth was ticking along just fine. But the truth was it was not. Something inside of me felt stuck and this 'stuckness' was playing out in my life. More specifically, I was feeling stuck in my work. Everything I seemed to be trying to do with my business was not flowing and it felt increasingly as if I was pushing water upstream. I became aware my passion for what I was doing in relation to raising self-esteem with youth was not what it had been.

Maybe it was time for something new. Perhaps it was time for a new stepping stone to reveal itself.

~

The breakthrough came during an impromptu coaching session with a fellow coach and dear friend. We were focusing on the 'stuckness' of my work and as is the way when someone listens deeply and asks the right questions, in a light bulb moment of clarity I saw I needed to write my story. This awareness had been bubbling around for a while but I had pushed it away probably through fear and lack of self-belief. The thought of writing a book seemed too big but I know **it is often the way, we stand at the bottom of a mountain and look up and are overwhelmed by the magnitude of the journey.**[2] As a result of this there are so many journeys we never embark on, so many adventures we never have, that would invariably be to our benefit.

It seemed that again life was asking me to step up to the challenge and set out on the journey of writing my story; sharing what I had learnt from the experiences and wounds that life had gifted me. 'Toddler steps Miguel' I told myself 'focus on each step one at a time. Stay focused and present and the journey will take care of itself.'

People had been telling me for quite some time my story was unusual and inspiring and would be of interest to others. I suppose I have packed quite a few adventures into my forty three years and I really saw, for the first time that day, if by sharing my story I could connect with others and perhaps inspire them a little too, then it would be selfish of me not to write. It is strange how we can keep being told the same thing and not really hear it until we are ready. I sometimes refer to this as ripeness. **Although we may have been told the same thing many times it is not until we are ripe to hear the words they really make an impact.**[3] It would appear I was ripe and the time for me to write my book had arrived.

When things are happening as they are meant to sometimes little incidents occur that seem to confirm you are on the right track.[4] Two such incidents happened on the same day I made the decision to begin writing. The first was when I picked up a book in my friend's kitchen; it was called The Millionaire Messenger by Brendon Burchard, and was all about sharing one's story and gifts of experience and learning in order to make a living. It is not that I would like to be a millionaire, I have no need of so much money but I would like to live comfortably. The idea of making a living by sharing what I have learnt from my journey of healing had never really entered my consciousness until that coaching session. Bumping into The Millionaire Messenger seemed to be a sign that I should write my own story and later that day something else happened to confirm this. I shared my idea to write my autobiography with my friends on Facebook; to my amazement one of my friends responded by saying I should read the book The Millionaire Messenger! I had never heard of this book before and on the same day I realised I needed to write my book, it was popping up all over the place! To some this may have been coincidence but to me it was confirmation I needed to sit down and write.

I didn't have much work booked so it seemed the perfect time to dedicate to my new venture and I began. As I began to write I received emails and texts of support from friends. My Dad and sister kindly offered to lend me some money so I could relax and get into a creative flow without the worry of my financial situation bothering me. It was beautiful how it all just came together. My experience is **when we are doing what is in**

alignment with what we are meant to be doing, things fall into place and flow.[5]

It feels the right time to be writing this book because everything has come into alignment in my life. If I had written it earlier there would have been no natural ending and, in reality, there is no definitive ending to my story as I expect to live and learn for many years to come. I believe that this life time is but one chapter in the story of something larger than Miguel. I have reached a pivotal point in this life which feels as if everything has been conspiring for me to arrive at. This book is the culmination of this process of alignment but there are two other things I need to share with you to put this completely into context.

~

I made the decision to book myself onto the next New Warrior training weekend with The Mankind Project. Interestingly, the moment I made the decision my feeling of 'stuckness' began to diminish. I began to write my book and then my soul mate entered my life. Her name is Katrina and she is beautiful in every way. We had met briefly at a Non-Violent Communication workshop a few months earlier and had kept in touch loosely. Eventually we had agreed to meet up for a coffee and as I was still seeing Linda at the time I tried my best to convince myself this was not a date but a networking meeting. However, when we did meet it was clear there was a mutual attraction. I had told Linda I was meeting Katrina and the next day when I saw Linda I told her what had happened. It was the final straw for Linda and she ended our relationship there and then. I do not blame her; it was the right thing to do. It was clear to her our journey together was over. I wish I had

had the courage to walk away earlier but perhaps it needed to be this way, perhaps she needed to have the final say.

Katrina and I met a few times and I knew from the start this was something different. It wasn't a fairytale love at first sight affair but this in itself was a good sign, as with all the significant women in my life my feelings have grown steadily and my perception of their beauty has grown with time too. I knew that before I could wholly commit to opening my wounded heart to this woman I had work to do in order to finally delete my old programming around my fear of loving fully and allowing myself to be loved. I had vowed that I would not get involved with another woman through fear of being alone and that I had to let go of my fear of opening my heart once and for all.

~

The time was right and I was booked on the Mankind Project weekend which I just knew was the right place for this healing work to be done. I do not need to say too much about my experience on the weekend but suffice to say that it did the job! It was an incredibly powerful experience. It was an ordeal. It was beautiful. It was deeply touching. There were eighty men present, half were initiates and half were staff. The powerful and safe container of so many wonderful men meant it was easy for me to go straight into that place within me where the grief around the death of my mother still lay. Held lovingly in the arms of another man I wept and wept until there was no grief left inside me. This massive emotional release was followed by waves of beautiful energy which coursed through my body and surfaced in the form of uncontrollable laughter. An amazing feeling of release and liberation followed and a sense of utter exhaustion. My work was done. I knew I had needed to let go of this grief that had remained with me for forty two years of my life and that now I was free to stand fully in my own power. For the first time in my life I did not have a numb feeling around my heart. For the first time I felt an openness and expansiveness in my chest. For the first time I did not feel like a boy in a man's body but I felt integrated and whole.

~

I will need to be aware of issues around commitment and women and not allow old fears to resurface to start sabotaging my relationship with Katrina. I know it is no coincidence this woman arrived in my life when she did. She arrived at exactly the right time; for I am now a man who can fully allow myself to love and be loved without fear. When I look at Katrina I see a woman I want to walk with me on the next part of this amazing journey through life. I want her to meet my family and friends. I want to show her off and I have never felt this about a woman before. I am proud she has chosen me to be her man and I am very proud to have her as my woman.

It's not that having a good woman to love is the be all and end all, but for me it felt like the end of a forty two year journey. The death of my mother set in motion a quest for me to find the courage within me to open my heart and risk being abandoned and left again; to risk opening my heart knowing that unless my heart was open I would not be able to enjoy the ultimate experience of deep connection with another human being. It feels that healing this wound has been a large part of my life's work and although I know there is more for me to learn in this lifetime I cannot begin to describe the huge relief this piece of work has now been done.

It feels fitting I should complete my writing today as it is the Summer Solstice; the longest day of the year when there is most light and least darkness. Summer Solstice is a time of abundant sun energy and for thousands of years the sun has been recognised as the ultimate symbol of the sacred masculine. Within me I can feel the strength of the man I have become - and it feels good!

Lessons for Life

1. People come and go in our lives and their presence always brings a gift or a lesson of some shape or form.

2. It is often the way that we stand at the bottom of a mountain and look up and are overwhelmed by the magnitude of the journey.

3. Although we may have been told the same thing many times it is not until we are ripe to hear the words that they really make an impact.

4. When things are happening as they are meant to sometimes little incidents occur that seem to confirm you are on the right tracks.

5. When we are doing what is in alignment with what we are meant to do be doing things fall into place and flow.

Epilogue

I am an ordinary man that has certainly not overcome the world's biggest challenges. I have heard of many people who have endured and overcome much more than I ever have or will do.

I hope that every man or woman who reads this book will see they are not alone in the struggles that they face. We all face challenges, as I have done; challenges of death and illness and separation and loss and the challenge to find meaning and purpose in our lives.

It is the challenges and wounds that somehow bring us together to unite us in our humanity. It is our suffering that gives us compassion and empathy and it is these qualities that enable us to connect with our fellow human beings. This connection, with an open heart, is the greatest gift of life.

I am fully aware that life is an on-going journey of healing. My body is still out of balance from the drugs I took for the Hepatitis. I do my best to cope with the discomfort this causes and know that complete health and wellbeing gets closer every day while I focus on a holistic approach to health. Jealousy and insecurity still raise their heads now and again and I must remain vigilant not to allow fear to sneak in and sabotage my relationship with Katrina.

Whatever lies ahead, at least I now know I have shared my story with you - so far. Through writing I have come to fully appreciate how rich and full my life has been and is - by reading it, I hope you may be able to see the beauty in your life and understand how pain inevitably will play a part too. If I seem to have dwelled on some of the darker parts of my life it is because from those times of darkness I have learnt the most. I have come to realise my power and have developed deep compassion, mostly as a result of these darker times. In my life I have also experienced much joy and beauty and I feel these qualities can only now be fully relished with the open and healed heart I now have. Every experience I have had has led me to the exact moment where I am now. If, as a result of these experiences and the subsequent learning, I can help you through some of your challenges and support your growth then I am grateful for all of it.

Ralph Waldo Emerson once said:

'What lies behind us and what lies before us are tiny matters compared with what lies within us.'

What lies within me is a growing sense of health, strength and purpose. When the time is right the mist will clear and I will see the next step to take. 'Whether in the mist or in the clear I shall continue to remain open and loving for I know that this is the best way to be ready to receive the gifts in the adversity that lies ahead...'

Visit www.steppingstonesinthemist.com

And enter your email in the box

1. To receive your free top ten tips on overcoming adversity

2. To arrange a one to one consultation (telephone/Skype)

3. For information on Overcoming Adversity talks and workshops

About The Author

Miguel Dean was born in England in 1968. The sudden death of his mother led to a tumultuous childhood and on leaving home he soon found himself immersed in an underworld of drugs and violence. The arrival of his son was the pivotal point which led him to take stock of his life and begin to take responsibility for where he was headed.

From this point on he began a journey of transformation, healing and self- discovery. Work in the homeless sector and in further education eventually led to him making the transition to self-employment where he felt he was best placed to live a life where he no longer had to compromise his values. He continues to learn from life's more recent challenges such as illness and divorce and lives by the mantra that it is not so much what happens to us in life but how we respond to what happens that makes the difference.

Miguel's request to you:

I would rather that this book does not gather dust on a shelf when you have read it. My intention is that the healing potential woven into its' fabric be shared and touch as many lives as possible.

Please pass it on.

Thank you.